THE PRESENTATION OF CASE MATERIAL IN CLINICAL DISCOURSE

Papers presented at the Freud Museum Conference September 23rd and 24th 1995.

edited by Ivan Ward

Address for correspondence
20 Maresfield Gardens, London NW3 5SX

Cover photo shows a detail of *Une Leçon Clinique à la Salpêtrière* by André Brouillet (1857-1914). A lithograph of this painting, from which the image is taken, hangs above the couch in Freud's consulting room.

20 Maresfield Gardens, London NW3 5SX

ISBN: 0 948687 10 X

Designed and typeset by Ivan Ward

Printed by Printek, Northampton, England

CONTENTS

Introduction

Ivan Ward

It still strikes me myself as strange that the case histories I write should read like short stories and that, one might say, they lack the serious stamp of science.
Sigmund Freud, *Studies on Hysteria*

The essays in this book consider an issue often neglected, or even avoided, in psychoanalysis - the way psychoanalysis itself is communicated. In particular they focus on the presentation of case material in psychoanalytic writing, or what I have called 'clinical discourse'.

Most examples of clinical discourse interweave psychoanalytic theory with analytic material from sessions. The author is looking to paint a realistic clinical picture and understand it in theoretical terms; and the strands of the text are held together through the techniques and style of writing.

By 'theory', I mean not only the concepts but also the premises and basic assumptions of the theory being used. Different analytic approaches make different assumptions about the role of the past, sexuality, object relations and so on, which will influence the way phenomena are described and the relative importance of specific concepts. 'Analytic material' includes not only the words and life history of the patient but also the words of the analyst and other elements of the analytic situation which are written up. While 'writing' comprises the tropes, metaphors and narrative structures that are instrumental in constructing any text. That is to say, the case report has qualities of a literary genre; it is not a simple window on the analytic world. All this I think is obvious, if a little simplistic.

Case presentations also represent or put in place significant relationships: a *therapist* is describing a *patient* to an *audience*. Each of these positions is graphically represented in the lithograph which hangs above Freud's couch at the Freud Museum, *La Leçon du Dr Charcot*, with the great doctor displaying the patient Blanche Wittman to the assembled audience[1]. In the case of analytic discourse the patient remains invisible and something of the words she has uttered in the privacy of analysis will be transmitted to the audience. Blanche Wittman achieved celebrity status in her day as a public figure and famous patient; analytic writing is constrained by the necessary requirement of confidentiality (See Susan Budd's paper).

The audience itself is an important factor in case presentations. They may be students in a subordinate position to a supervisor, colleagues in a peer relationship, or teachers occupying a dominant position. These relationships exert subtle pressures on the way case material is presented and initially selected (See Ron Britton's paper). In the process of selection the therapist *reassembles* the patient's discourse. He does not just repeat the patient's words but adds to them with his own and creates something new, a case history, which attempts to integrate the material of the clinical encounter into the 'single story of suffering', as Freud called it, of the patient's life. Even today many analysts argue that creating meaningful sequences between disparate events in a person's life - a story - is an important part of psychoanalysis. But Freud was faced with a dilemma. On the one hand he wanted to write a compelling story that had the ring of emotional truth about it. On the other hand he wanted to produce scientific knowledge based on a technique of free association which undermines the telling of stories. The problem of the case history, for Freud, is the problem of communicating the fine texture of analytic experience as a form of scientific evidence.

It might be useful, if once again simplistic, to say that the therapist constructs three things in his writing: a *story*, a *description*, and a *theory*, which is offered to the reader. Sometimes the demands of the theory will interfere with the requirements of a good story (including dialogue between the characters). At other times it will be the other way round. In many cases the three elements are clearly separated in the text; a theoretical proposition is advanced and a clinical vignette is introduced to illustrate it. This is what Laurence Spurling calls the 'ideological' function of the case presentation, and is still, I would suggest, the most common form in which case material is published. The clinical vignette is given to make the theory come alive in the real situation; indeed it often has precisely that effect on the reader. In much analytic writing clinical material is brilliantly described and illuminated. We, the readers, may be captivated by the experience and feel privileged to participate in the work even at second hand. We may be left with a sense of profound understanding that verges on the revelatory. Unfortunately such presentations have profound epistemological shortcomings. For every compelling interpretation of the material there are others, equally valid, which are obscured by the presentation (see Donald Spence's essay). It also, Spence argues, positions the therapist as the hero or heroine of a classic narrative, overcoming obstacles on the way to a pre-ordained resolution of the story. In a remarkable self-critical 'Commentary', Wilfred Bion made a similar point about his own earlier work. Through the 'fiction' of the narrative, he says, 'The reader is prepared for the triumph of psycho-analysis in contrast with the patient's previous misfortunes...' (W. R. Bion *Second Thoughts* p120, Karnac Books 1967). Bion evidently felt there was something misleading and unilluminating about the conventional presentation of cases.

To escape from some of these effects the therapist may relay his own subjective processes and internal dialogue. In this way he gives a sense of the vagaries of counter-transference and the uncertain process by which theoretical insights were arrived at. It also 'opens up' the text. If the therapist can escape from the omniscient, heroic mould to which he is confined by the classic narrative, the reader is encouraged to engage with the text in a more creative way. At least it gives an idea of the struggle involved in wrenching analytic understanding from recalcitrant material - there is an explicit gap between the patient's utterances and the therapist's interpretations - but it can also become ritualised and formulaic. Actually, the patient also has stories and descriptions and theories of his own, so the therapist is not the only creative one in this arrangement. The patient's stories, however, cease to be part of the patient's discourse when they are taken up in the process of the therapist's writing and theoretical concerns.

So the case history, as a literary text, contains a set of implied relationships between therapist, patient and audience. Within this form one could say that the therapist writes *himself* up. He becomes a psychotherapist-for-others. Like the writing up of fieldwork in social anthropology the case history functions as a rite of passage in the process of assuming a professional identity. The neophyte takes on the mantle of a particular discourse through a dynamic interplay of mimicry, projection and identification. In the process of writing he smooths over the rough edges of experience and recreates it in a different form. Nevertheless, both the psychoanalyst and anthropologist claim a priviledged understanding of the material based on their concrete *experience* of fieldwork or therapy. This might seem reasonable. However the history of anthropology is littered with cases of fieldworkers simply getting it wrong[2], and Julia Borossa investigates the legitimacy of the claim in her essay.

Writing about the other person or the other culture can be instrumental, therefore, in constructing an identity. The difficulty is in remembering who we were - that 'I have not always been a psychotherapist', as Freud once said (Freud and Breuer *Studies on Hysteria* S.E. 2, p160). The discourse and the institutions, however, may conspire against remembering by representing the psychotherapist in certain ways.

Let me take one example of what I am talking about. I have often been struck, when listening to lectures on psychoanalysis, at the number of times the audience laughed at a description of a patient. This was often the case with, say, the description of the behaviour of an obsessional person, forever washing his hands or checking for the umpteenth time whether the gas was turned off. I took this laughter to mean either that the audience felt themselves as quite different from the patient under discussion, or that they felt uncomfortably close and used the laughter in order to distance themselves.

It seemed to me that in either case the laughter opposed itself to Freud's ambition to close the 'supposed gap' between normal and pathological behaviour. To this end Freud used a number of rhetorical strategies; when he talks about 'normal' jealousy he is quick to point out that it may be normal but it is far from rational. When he talks about perversion he is at pains to argue that the disposition to perversions of all sorts is a fundamental characteristic of human sexuality, and so on. In fact the diagnostic categories that therapists use to define patients were used by Freud to define normal phenomena as well. So art is a bit like hysteria, science is a bit like paranoia and religion is a bit like an obsessional neurosis - with its repetitive rituals and anxieties about getting things wrong. This laughter, then, was an indication of the structure of a discourse - or at least of the case history presentation. In many cases the presenter of the case material - a psychoanalyst perhaps - would be embarrassed at the evoked reaction. She would make amends by interrupting her prepared talk and commenting on the laughter; or she would remind her audience of the mental pain the patient was in fact suffering from, thus shaming them into silence. Such use of a 'meta-discourse' is not always possible in larger gatherings.

Then I heard an alternative way of presenting clinical material which seemed to address the fundamental dynamic of the 'case presentation' itself. It was a lecture by Adam Limentani 'On the psychodynamics of drug dependence' (in *Between Freud and Klein*, Free Association Books, 1989). As I remember it, and the effect at the time was electric, most of the lecture consisted of reading out a 'letter' he had received from a former patient. By this simple gesture Limentani opened up new possibilities of how case material and patients can be presented. In the first place the patient was represented as speaking for himself. In the second place Limentani put himself in the position of the patient by reading out a letter in the first person. Thirdly he did this in the presence of an audience, to himself. These manoeuvres transformed the structure of the discourse and the relative positions within it. Nobody laughed, except when the letter-writer cracked a joke. The patient was allowed to occupy a quite different place in the clinical discourse and the audience perceived the material and the analytic situation in a new light. The patient ceased being an object and became in some measure a subject - not so unlike the audience who were listening to his story. At the same time the security of the listener was disturbed; he could no longer assume a stable and dominant position within the discourse. As I say, the effect at the time was electric. Interestingly enough, the written form of this paper does not have the same impact, partly because the physical presence of the author himself is eliminated from the telling of the story. (We sometimes naively imagine that speaking and writing are more or less the same thing, but examples like this show our error. Patrick Mahony considers many of these issues in his book *Freud as a Writer*, Yale University Press 1987).

Much could be said about this simple example of a different way of doing things. It is by no means the only case of its kind, but nevertheless such examples are few and far between. In the following papers other strategies will be discussed, and other problems considered. We can only hope that the issues explored in these pages will enrich both our own understanding and, in a small way, the field of psychoanalysis itself.

Notes

1. Blanche Wittman herself became a pioneering radiographer at the same hospital and later died of cancer as a result. The lithograph was one of thousands produced from André Brouillet's huge painting *Une Leçon Clinique à la Salpêtrière* which now hangs in the neurological hospital at Lyon.

2. Even the most famous anthropologist of all, Margaret Mead, has been accused of writing little more than a wishful phantasy in her seminal work *The Coming of Age in Samoa*. (Freeman, D *Margaret Mead and Samoa* Cambridge Mass: Harvard University Press 1983). People often see only what they want to see, so 'experience' is a shaky foundation on which to build a scientific (as opposed to therapeutic) endeavour.

Making the Private Public

Ronald Britton

I am going to talk about the psychological problems associated specifically with the act of publication, whether spoken or written. I am not going to speak about difficulties in thinking and writing; nor about the complex, difficult and extremely important ethical issues involved in publishing clinical case material. Both these difficulties affect publication, obviously if someone cannot write they cannot publish; if they cannot satisfy themselves that it is ethical to publish what they have written they will not feel free to do so, and if it is not ethical then they should not do so. We have a duty to protect the anonymity of patients at all times and beyond that I believe we should seek the agreement of our patients before publishing direct clinical material obtained from their analyses even where there is nothing about it that anyone else could recognise.

I have found however that proceeding carefully by protecting the patient from recognition and securing the informed consent of the patient does not relieve us, as authors, of a sense of guilt. We may feel that we are not betraying a confidence but we are left with a feeling that we are betraying an affiliation. Nor does getting permission exonerate the analyst in the eyes of his patient and those who identify with the patient. The knowledge that had seemed to be the private possession of the analytic dyad has been shared with *others*: what had seemed to be the inter-subjective experience is offered as an object for their perusal; what had seemed like the mental content of a private relationship has become the raw material for other minds. The communications internal to one relationship have become the means of furthering the development of another relationship. In its most extreme form it feels best represented by the myth of Iphegenia whose father Agamemnon en route for the Trojan war sacrificed his daughter to get a fair wind from the gods and to propitiate his associates. And yet I also know that if I followed the example of some others and refrained from using analytic experience for writing I would feel I was betraying something else. In allegiance to a shared subjectivity, often these days referred to as inter-subjectivity, I would be betraying a commitment to an objectivity shared with professional colleagues past and present and with psychoanalysis itself. There are circumstances where objectivity is felt to be the death of subjectivity and others where subjectivity is felt to threaten the demise of objectivity.

This conflict between one allegiance and another is to be found inside an analysis when the analyst's empathic link with the patient's subjective world is felt to be threatened if he takes an objective view of it. The analyst's internal communication with that aspect of himself linked with his analytic ancestors and associates appears to confirm a conviction of childhood that one parent sacrificed a sympathetic understanding of the patient in order to remain united with the other parent. It is often the case where this conflict is particularly severe that there was support for this universal suspicion in the personal history of the patient. It is expressed in the Oedipus myth in Jocasta's readiness to sacrifice the life of her infant Oedipus to protect her husband. I have suggested in earlier papers that clinically this fear is likely to be more profound if the Oedipal situation was preceded by a problem of primary communication and containment between mother and infant.

Today I want to emphasise the ubiquity of these problems aroused by publication; the conflict between subjectivity and objectivity and its evocation of the Oedipal situation with its inevitable concomitants of anxiety, betrayal, guilt and shame.

In 1989 Ted Hughes, poet and husband of the late Sylvia Plath, wrote in a letter to the *Independent* 'I hope each of us owns the facts of our life'. He was provoked into writing this anguished comment by the growing literature about his dead wife, whose poetry and suicide had combined to give her a special place in the literary canon, and released a quantity of speculative and variously informed comment on their marriage and life together. 'But', comments Janet Malcolm in her book *The Silent Woman*, a refection on the Plath biographical enterprise, 'we do not own the facts of our lives at all. The real ownership passes out of our hands at birth, at the moment we are first observed'. This telling image of an infant observed I think resonates with the feelings aroused by the idea of the analyst who having been party to the emergence of undisclosed aspects of his patient is contemplating describing them as an observer to a third party.

This feeling in the analyst is perhaps somewhat offset in practice by the fact that when writing and contemplating publishing the analyst subjectively feels himself to be in a different situation: not that of one who exposes but one who is exposed. The tables are turned; now it is the private thoughts and opinions of the author that are about to be revealed not only to the desired object of his communication, that is the phantasied receptive audience, but also the observers of this attempted communication.

This description may sound familiar: of the analyst with conflicting claims for his mental allegiance; his patient's view of the world; his own, emergent view of it and the view he shares with his psychoanalytic affiliates. If it does it is probably because it echoes a passage in Freud's *Ego and the Id*. He wrote that 'we see this same ego as a poor creature owing service to three masters and consequently menaced by three dangers: from the external world, from the libido of the id, and from the severity of the super ego. Three kinds of anxiety correspond to these three dangers, since anxiety is the expression of a retreat from danger. As a frontier creature the ego tries to mediate between the world and the id....it behaves like the physician during analytic treatment: it offers itself, with the attention it pays to the real world, as a libidinal object to the id, and aims at attaching the id's libido to itself. It is not only a helper to the id; it is also a submissive slave who courts his master's love....In its position midway between the id and reality, it only too often yields to the temptation to become sycophantic, opportunist and lying, like a politician who sees the truth but wants to keep his place in popular favour'. (S.E. 19, p56)

This suggests there is an attachment to the truth and reality in all of us, that is to discovering *the way things are*, which conflicts with our own wishful thinking i.e. *the way we would like them to be*, and also it conflicts with beliefs based on morality, that is *the way we think things ought to be*. In other words the reality principle is always in conflict with the pleasure principle and its upmarket version the morality principle.

I would like to discuss the interplay of these forces by considering the difficulties people experience at the point of publication. The manifest problems in publication that I have found are that some people are afraid to publish, some are too ready to publish, and that in some others the conflicts inherent in publication lead to deviation, distraction or distortion of their texts. I believe that *publication anxiety* is natural unless it is denied as part of a manic defence which may lead to over-readiness to publish.

I think publication anxiety is ubiquitous and has two sources. One is fear of rejection by the primary intended audience. The other is fear of recrimination by affiliated colleagues and possible exile from them. I think that a profound *fear of rejection by the primary intended listener* in its most serious form leads to an inability to conceptualise or, in lesser states of inhibition, produces an inability to write. Even where this fear is relatively slight and there may be no inhibition in thinking and writing, there may be a significant fear of publication whether this is by public utterance or in written form. For the sake of clarity I call this second situation *publication anxiety*. It is *publication anxiety* that I want to discuss further; I think it emanates from a fear of criticism by third parties who are regarded as authoritative and *fear of disaffiliation* from colleagues with whom the author feels the need to be *affiliated*. This may result in a failure to publish written work or to speak publicly. Even if this inhibition is overcome it may still produce distortion or deviation within the text in the process of publication. If it is excessive it may cause inhibition, or if not it may result in distortion, deviation or distraction. If publication anxiety is denied the result is a superficial and complacent text. *Over-readiness to publish* which is not justified by the content of the text is familiar to editors of journals. I refer here to more than inadequacy of material, ideas or presentation but specifically to a blind sort of over-confident belief that whatever is said or written by the author deserves and will receive widespread approval; usually it is associated with banality. In the cases I am thinking of the phenomenon itself is a contributing cause to the poverty of the text rather than lack of ability in the author. It can therefore afflict previously successful writers or potentially talented authors. It is a form of intellectual complacency that can arise as part of a manic defence. It results from the unconscious phantasy of being the special representative of a superior power. This superior power is itself derived by the attributive projective identification of the phantasied omniscient self into an actual object, which might be a person or a school of thought. Such projective identification gives a sense of having a special connection to this power without having to claim omnipotence or omniscience for the self, thus preserving reality sense whilst retaining the belief in having access to oracular power. It may take the form of allegiance to an orthodoxy in which case the individual author has *a priestly function*. Or it may take an iconoclastic form in which the spirit of the new is felt to emanate from some intellectually respectable version of divine revelation in which case the author has *a prophetic function*.

In other cases complacency is derived from an incorporative identification in which the authority of an earlier author has been imbibed together with his ideas and absorbed into the thinking of the author not by intellectual assimilation but by a process which results in the disappearance of the intellectual debt to the original author and an illusion of originality. William Blake describes this phantasied incorporation of an earlier author in the prophetic book in which he claims that Milton entered his left foot making him the possessor of Milton's imagination. I have a colleague with a patient who entertains a similar idea that his visions of the truth are a result of wisdom entering him through his left foot. There is always an underlying precariousness in this intellectual structure, common though it is, because the derivation of the ideas is lacking and authority is only achieved by identification. Therefore any challenge leads simply to an assertion of authoritative identity: *I am therefore it is!*

I have already mentioned that I think the Oedipus situation is intrinsic to the problems of *publication anxiety*, I think therefore that

I should take a moment to explain what I mean by this term. In Melanie Klein's expanded concept (Klein 1928) in addition to Freud's positive and negative versions of the Oedipus complex, she included what he had referred to as the primal scene, i.e. the sexual relations of the parents as perceived and as imagined by the child. Thus, 'the Oedipus situation dawns with the child's recognition of the parents' relationship in whatever primitive or partial form; it is continued by the child's rivalry with one parent for the other, and is resolved by the child relinquishing his sexual claim on his parents by his acceptance of the reality of their sexual relationship' (Britton 1989).

From the beginning of her work in child analysis Klein emphasised the epistemophilic impulse, the customary translation of *Wissenstrieb*, the urge for knowledge, and stated that its fate was intimately connected with the epistemophilic aspects of the Oedipus situation. For the purposes of this discussion it is with the epistemophilic aspects of the Oedipus situation that I am concerned. Following Bion's use of L, H, and K, as designating the three links between psychic objects I think of three innate impulses as the bonds of all fundamental object relationships: the propensity to love, to hate, and to know. I have found it useful to be able to think of some clinical situations as resulting not from a conflict between love and hate but between the desire to love and the desire to know: situations where further knowledge of an object has been thought to be incompatible with continuing to love it. Similarly I have found conflict between hate and knowledge where there is a wish to be free of any actual knowledge of the object which might restrict the capacity to hate unconditionally.

The full Oedipus situation, as I conceive it following Bion's description of L H and K, has all three impulses forming potential links between all three members of the triangle. I believe that new discoveries, however modest, evoke, once again, the Oedipus situation. Gaining knowledge of an object engenders in the individual a sense of possessing it and thus it evokes anxiety lest this will provoke retaliation from a third party: publication advertises possession of the knowledge.

The particular anxieties evoked will be influenced by the intellectual context in which the author's findings emerge. That is in the state of *the central organizing theory* coined by Kuhn, for this central theory organises and legitimises every scientific discipline or subdiscipline. I find Kuhn's account of the nature of scientific development convincing in his *Structure of Scientific Revolutions* (Kuhn 1962) and I think it applies in microcosm to psychoanalysis. He describes different phases, in a natural cycle of scientific development. He suggests that a science moves from the establishment of a new *paradigm*, through a period of its development and application to its destabilisation by the accumulation of anomalies; this is followed by its dissolution in favour of a new paradigm. The publication anxieties of the writer are inevitably influenced by the phase of this cycle that his new science is in at the time. Whether it is in a phase characterised by confirmation, confidence, and coherence, or a phase characterised by discrepancy, doubt, and fragmentation.

Kuhn suggests that 'normal science' begins when a 'paradigm' is established and provides the definition by which the science is judged (Kuhn 1962, p10). 'Normal science' includes accumulating relevant facts, addressing puzzles, and making discoveries (ibid. p37). Discovery however creates problems because it reveals anomalies in the paradigm, the central theory itself. Anomalies accumulate until the new theories they generate fragment the paradigm leaving the scientific discipline concerned in confusion and uncertainty until a new paradigm emerges which redefines 'normal science'. Kuhn observes that 'the emergence of new theories is generally preceded by a period of pronounced professional insecurity' (ibid. p67,68).

The point in Kuhn's cycle therefore that is likely to be associated with maximal publication anxiety is when *anomalies* have accumulated in the subject and *destabilised* the existing paradigm, or when the state of the science requires the integration of previously segregated theories or facts. I mention this because I think that within our own discipline the pressure to integrate the theories of the different schools of psychoanalytic thought means that we are in a period characterised by of destabilisation of previously confidently held psychoanalytic paradigms.

At this point in the cycle the scientific writer most fears that his publication may damage the authority of the guardians of the paradigm, and demoralise his affiliates (depressive anxiety), or he may fear the wrath of the guardians and his exile from his affiliates (persecutory anxiety). This I see as cast in the mould of the Oedipus situation. The writer wishes to publish his view of his primary (scientific) object. He would like his version of this object to be unique because this would give him possession of it; he alone would know *the truth* of the object. On the other hand he desires the approval of his ancestors and to be at one with his scientific affiliates, his scientific family, who have their own view of this object. The optimal compromise is to claim *a share of the truth* by making an individual contribution that adds to the total truth and at the same time affiliates him with his fellows in their shared knowledge.

This compromise is tenable during the phase of what Kuhn calls 'normal science'. When the paradigm is no longer satisfactory, the author who publishes new facts fears that he may be the messenger with bad news and the worker who publishes a new theory feels that he risks destroying his own subject or alienating himself from his scientific home. At an earlier point in the cycle when the paradigm is authoritative and appears infinitely extendable, publication is easier for those who are happy simply adding 'facts' to expand, exemplify and refine it. This is the phase of 'normal science'. However for more restless, ambitious, or determinedly original spirits the fear in this phase is that they will not find creative space for themselves.

This problem, as applied to poetry, was addressed, in terms of the Oedipal situation, by Harold Bloom in his concept of 'the anxiety of influence'. He described this as the fear in a poet that a dominant predecessor (such as Milton) had already taken total possession of the field from which the emerging poet hoped would come his own potential poetry (Bloom H. 1973). That the predecessor had said the last word on the subject. 'The 'belated poet's' attitudes to his precursor...are ambivalent...compounded not only of love and admiration but also of hate, envy and fear of the father poet's pre-emption of the son's imaginative space...(He) safeguards his own sense of autonomy and priority by reading a parent-poem defensively, in such a way as to distort it beyond his own conscious recognition. Nonetheless, he cannot avoid embodying the malformed parent-poem into his own doomed attempt to write an unprecedented original poem; the most that even the best belated poet can achieve is to write a poem so 'strong' that it effects an illusory priority' (Abrams M. H. 1957 p82).

This *anxiety of influence,* judging from his letters, in 1952, was what Donald Winnicott felt in relation to Melanie Klein in the aftermath of her production of a new paradigm, the theory of the paranoid-schizoid and depressive positions. A new generation of analysts clustered around this paradigm rapidly applying it and utilising it; they became known as *the Kleinians*. Winnicott suggested in a letter sent jointly to Anna Freud and Melanie Klein that 'rigid patterns... create iconoclasts or claustrophobics' and added 'perhaps I am one of them' (Rodman 1987 p72). He wrote to Klein in November 1952:

> *I personally think that it is very important that your work should be restated by people discovering in their own way and presenting what they discover in their own language* (ibid. p34).

Later (Feb 3 1956) he wrote to Joan Rivière, his former analyst and Klein's most authoritative ally, to complain:

> *You and she spoke to me and within the framework of friendliness you gave me to understand that both of you are absolutely certain that there is no positive contribution to be made from me to the interesting attempt Melanie is making all the time to state the psychology of the earliest stages. You will agree that you implied that the trouble is that I am unable to recognise that Melanie does say the very things that I am asking her to say. In other words, there is a block in me* (ibid. p94).

He added a sentence which makes the point I made earlier about fear of exile:

> *If I contribute to psychoanalytic theory, it is not of course necessary for me to be accepted by either yourself or Melanie Klein, but I do in fact mind tremendously if I really have a positive contribution to make, however small, and if this cannot find acceptance either with you or with Melanie* (ibid. p96).

Winnicott did not have a 'following' at this time and asked Anna Freud if she could provide an audience for a paper he proposed to write. This was to be critical of what he called 'Mrs Klein's temporary (I hope) insistence on what she calls innate envy, something which involves the idea of a variable genetic factor' (ibid. p93). To publish this challenge he needed, apparently, a supporting power to neutralise the rejection he feared from his former authorities:

> *I am writing to you because I am wondering whether you have a group that I could write this short paper for so that it could be discussed. I would be quite contented, of course, if you were to*

> *say that it would be best if I were to write it and send it to you...I need an audience of at least one so that I may orientate to the presentation of my idea.* (ibid. p94)

He did not appear to see, however, that Klein might feel the need of a group of adherents to confront the hostile opposition to her ideas that she was encountering. In his letter condemning 'Kleinianism' and begging her to 'destroy it' he implicitly compares her to Darwin and Kleinians to Darwinians. As I describe below, Darwin needed a group of followers before he could bring himself to publish his theories. Winnicott wrote to her:

> *I have no difficulty whatever in telling anyone who asks me, from the bottom of my heart, that you are the best analyst as well as the most creative in the analytic movement. What you do not meet, however, is the opposition to Kleinism which I used to think was simply an invention of Glover's but which I now have to admit exists as something which is as much a barrier to the growth of scientific thought in the Society as Darwinism was to the growth in biology greatly stimulated by the work of Darwin himself* (ibid p.37).

Darwin would not have seen it like that, though made anxious by the fervour of his followers such as T. H. Huxley, he relied on the support of the Darwinians.

I would like to take Charles Darwin and the long delayed publication of his theory of evolution as an illustration of the situation where in a context of changing science and anomalous facts, an author suffers acute publication anxiety and consequent inhibition. Darwin's new paradigmatic theory of evolution arose, in Kuhn's terms, when the 'normal science' of Natural History was finding too many anomalous facts to be contained within its general theory. His theory fascinated him; the idea of publishing it terrified him. It was several years before he wrote even a pencil sketch of the theory, and seventeen years after he had written it, when it was finally to be published as a book, he still wanted to call it *An Abstract of an Essay on the Origin of Species and Varieties through Natural Selection*. His publisher Murray knew his trade well enough to produce it under the title *The Origin of Species*. However, under the influence of Darwin's pessimism and diffidence, he published only five hundred copies. Even to the last, Darwin asked his friend and disciple Lyell, 'would you advise me to tell

Murray that my book is not more unorthodox than the subject makes inevitable?'

We have an amazingly bold thinker who was tormented by the thought of publishing his theories and convinced of catastrophe for himself, and everyone else important to him, if he did so. He suffered greatly from neurotic symptoms, depression, and psychosomatic ill health which fluctuated wildly in keeping with his fears of publication and its consequences. The threads of the conflict are evident in his letters and journals from the moment of the germination of his ideas during the voyage of the Beagle.

Darwin came from a historically freethinking family, but he lived in and was educated in a society that had reverted to religious orthodoxy in belief and piety in practice. He was supposed to join that body of professional Naturalists who were at the same time members of the Anglican Clergy. Though evolution was touted by radicals in England, it was not thought tenable by the Naturalist Establishment from which Darwin drew his scientific sustenance. Even if evolution was to be accepted in place of orthodox creationism, some form of recurrent acts of creation were thought of by such a dominant figure in biology as Owen. The people Darwin learned from and admired were very good scientists within their own definition, this in a very English way, meant precise work, painstaking collection, mastery of detail and abhorrence of general ideas. Darwin, secretly developing his ideas and anticipating severe criticism, prepared himself by becoming the greatest collector of specimens, finder of facts, and examiner of detail, imaginable. He needed to do all this work, not to provide himself with ideas, but to substantiate the ones he already had. He published these accounts of his detailed work and careful observations and earned a considerable reputation as a consequence, but his general theory of evolution which they were meant to illustrate remained totally private until he had a potential disciple, Joseph Hooker.

From the beginnings of his career in research on the voyage of the Beagle, he was ambivalent about his findings and the scientific ideas they generated in him. He was isolated from scientific colleagues and making findings increasingly discrepant from the orthodox views in geology, paleontology and biology. On the one hand, he entertained fantasies of great discoveries; on the other, he feared that a word of scientific disapproval from Henslow, his scientific paterfamilias, would finish him. When he wrote to Henslow in 1835, he told of his incredible scientific findings and making no mention of theory swore that 'no previously formed conjecture warped my judgement' (Desmond A. and Moore J. 1992 p165). To his father and sisters, however, he boasted that his findings would be crucial 'to the theory of the formation of the world' (ibid. p165). In 1836 whilst still waiting to know the response to his notes, he wrote:

> *I look forward with no little anxiety to the time when Henslow, putting on a grave face, shall decide on the merits of my notes. If he shakes his head in a disapproving manner: I shall then know I had better at once give up science, for science will have given me up* (ibid p183).

In the event Henslow's response was enthusiastic. Darwin became increasingly successful in his scientific work, married happily but remained sick with worry. He was steadily collecting every sort of fact 'which may throw light on the origin and variation of species'. In 1839 his ideas were advancing, his conviction growing, his anxiety increasing: his findings and theories would have been music to the ears of street atheists, but not of course to Henslow (ibid. p286). In May 1842, he produced a thirty-five page sketch of his evolutionary theory in pencil. In late 1843 and early 1844 he confessed to Joseph Hooker that:

> *I am almost convinced quite contrary to the opinion I started with that species are not (it is like confessing a murder) immutable* (ibid. p314).

Relieved by Hooker's non-hostile, and interested response, he expanded his sketch into a full 189 page essay. Despite the growth of a circle of followers around him, this essay remained unpublished and he was only pushed into doing anything with it in 1858 by the sickening news that Wallace had produced something like his long cherished theory of Natural Selection. Prompted by this, he allowed his friends and supporters Hooker and Lyell to make his theory public at the carefully chosen, relatively small, Linnaean Society. There at a regular scientific meeting they read extracts from his essay, part of a letter Darwin sent to Gray on the subject, and Wallace's paper to a largely uncomprehending audience. Finally, a year later, in November 1859, there was the actual publication: Darwin called it 'the appearance of my child'. He wrote in anxious anticipation to Henslow, 'I fear you will not approve of your pupil' and to other respected colleagues he wrote such sentences as 'you will fulminate anathemas', 'Lord, how savage you will be...how you will crucify me alive' or '[to you] it will seem like an abomination' (ibid. p476)

He had two fears of the consequences of publication. One was that the scientific establishment which had raised him would destroy him, the other was that he would be responsible for the triumph of anarchy over authority and the consequent destruction of society. It seems clear that Darwin was powerfully prompted from within to reveal that he knew the secrets of the origin of the world which his scientific fathers did not. His ideas fascinated him but any thought of publishing them made him feel ill. It was not until he was bolstered by a band of junior siblings that he exposed his theory and even then, the fear of the fathers remained. Darwin, however, did not compromise in his thinking and there was no distortion in his text to facilitate affiliation. The one misrepresentation was that he wanted it believed that he was forced, against his wishes and previous convictions, reluctantly and slowly, to his conclusions by accumulated evidence. In reality, his enormous research efforts were to test his theory; to provide irrefutable evidence for it and to protect himself from any imputation of being scientifically speculative.

I would like to turn from complete inhibition of publication to consider the possible effects of the same forces in producing *distortions* within the published text. What I have in mind is the distracting or distorting effects on direct communication arising from the wish to further or preserve affiliation with the significant peer group or parental figure. To illustrate what I mean I would first like to use a portion of an important paper by Karl Abraham 'A short study of the development of the libido, viewed in the light of the mental disorders' (Abraham 1924). I have chosen this because it is a publication of an analyst I unequivocally admire for his straightforwardness and his independent thinking and who, even so, when describing an important anomaly or discovery, is led by anxiety to wobble, and weaken his text.

Abraham was writing 'Notes on the Psychogenesis of Melancholia' which was very much his own subject. He, unlike Freud, had analysed a number of manic-depressive patients and shared his findings with Freud who doubtless used them in his won ground-breaking papers 'Mourning and Melancholia' and *The Ego and the Id*. Nevertheless, at the time that Abraham was writing his paper, the Castration complex and the Father complex were very much in the ascendent in Freud's theorising e.g. 'A Seventeenth Century Demonological Neurosis' (Freud 1923a) and 'The Infantile Genital Organization: An Interpolation into the Theory of Sexuality' (Freud 1923b). Abraham was, however, about to say that he thought the whole psychological process in melancholia centred around the mother, and a few paragraphs later was to say 'If we want to realise the full strength of the melancholiac's hostility toward his mother, and to understand the particular character of his castration complex, we must keep in mind Stärcke's theory that the withdrawal of the mother's breast is a 'primal castration''. In this paper Abraham was about to shift the psychoanalytic ground on which subsequent understanding of depressive states of mind would be understood and thus he threatened the prevailing paradigm. I think we can detect anxiety about this with a risk of distortion in the text from which he appeared to recover but lost some directness and force in the process. I would suggest certain phrases were used for their totemic significance in furthering affiliation with Freud. There is, just after the passage that implies that the introjected mother forms the feared super-ego rather than the father, a distinctly placatory footnote deferring to Freud. Abraham began with the claim:

> *In every male melancholic I have hitherto analysed I have been able to satisfy myself that the patient's castration complex was quite predominantly connected with his mother, whereas in other kinds of patients it is usually much more in evidence in relation to the father* (ibid. p406).

Then he qualified this:

> *Nevertheless I was able to discover that its connection with the mother was a secondary one and the result of a tendency to invert the Oedipus situation. When thoroughly analysed the hostility of the melancholic towards his mother is seen to have roots in the Oedipus complex. In fact, his ambivalence really applies to both parents alike. And his father is also the object of a process of introjection. Many melancholic symptoms, as, for instance, certain self-reproaches, show their original relation to both parents quite clearly* (ibid. p460-1).

He reasserts his claim:

> *What I have just said does not invalidate my previous statement that in melancholia the whole psychological process centres* in the male *round the mother; it only seeks to emphasise the fact that the process has more than one determinant* (ibid. p461).

He went on to make quite clear that the 'ego-ideal' is built on the introjected original love-object, the mother, quoting the patient as using her tone of voice and expressions. It is in this paragraph in which the concept of the super-ego as heir to the classical Oedipus complex is most in question that he used the deferential footnote as below:

> *1. The patient has introjected his original love-object upon which he had built his ego ideal; so that object has taken over the role of conscience for him, although, it is true, a pathologically formed one. Our material goes to show that the pathological self-criticism of the melancholic emanates from this introjected object.**
>
> [Footnote] * *Freud's* The Ego and the Id *appeared shortly after I had written this part of my book. In it he gives such a lucid account of the process that I need only refer the reader to its pages. To give a resumé of it would be to render it less clear* (ibid. p461).

This paper was clearly addressed to the 'reader' and Freud's presence in Abraham's mind and in the text at these points served as a distraction. It is, I think, of some significance that the primary importance of the father was almost reinstated in the text and the supremacy of the castration complex implied at a moment when Abraham's thinking was clearly moving in another direction. I point this out not to criticise Abraham or indict Freud, but to give an example of what I think may be omnipresent in our publications. Small distortions, totemic use of terms, detours into irrelevant references, links made with other works not clearly connected to the thesis; all prompted by our desire for affiliation and our fear of exile.

As a final illustration of this, where less important issues are at stake but the same dynamic is operating, I take a short passage from the beginning of a fairly recent paper, read to the 'Kleinian Studies Group' of the British Society in 1983.

The author began by describing a situation in analysis where a patient has rid himself of knowledge and feeling by projective identification. The author was about to raise, in his paper, the possible implications of this for a change of analytic technique in such clinical situations. He began by describing the clinical dilemma: 'the knowledge born of previous experience in the analysis may now only have a home in the analyst. If this knowledge is of the existence of a person capable of love and desirous of communication now apparently only existing in the analyst's mind, his own loneliness or frustration may prompt him to demand the patient admits it, or he may be tempted to try and sell it to the patient'.

We then had a distraction in terms of an ancestral reference:

> *'Perhaps'*, he wrote, *'it was situations like this which prompted Bion to enjoin us to forfeit memory and desire in order to discern the current state in the analysis.'*

He then put forward his argument:

> *Paradoxically however the situation would seem to depend at these moments on the analyst's secure containment of his own unspoken knowledge and reality. This, I think, fluctuates with our capacity to sustain our point of view without need of the patient's confirmation or acquiescence thus leaving us free to make* explicit *the patient's view of things leaving our own position* implicit *in our ability and readiness to do so.*

The next two paragraphs muddied the waters however because reference was made to clarifying a number of situations that might arise as a consequence of 'splitting', 'evacuation', 'fragmentation', 'annihilation' and 'omnipotent phantasy'. The flow of the idea had been interrupted but no one could doubt that it was a Kleinian paper after that barrage. In the process the author also managed to mention contributions by Rosenfeld, Joseph, and Segal in the space of ten lines. The resumption of the argument in the paper was, therefore, less clear than it would have been.

I would not be so free with my comments if I were not the author in question, which is why I chose one of my own for scrutiny. The idea put forward in the paper found its way into print six years later, 1989, in a larger context, without the diversion of the irrelevant affiliative references to ancestral figures. However, when I was publicising this idea of mine in 1983, anxious to bind myself to my ancestors and affiliates, I succeeded in distracting myself and probably everyone else, by alluding to a number of familiar shared concepts and mentioning one principle ancestral figure and all three of my analytic supervisors in just twenty lines.

I offer this as a commonplace example of publication anxiety which results in the sort of genuflection to be found in many papers. There are more serious distortions that can occur in texts where affirmation of shared ideas, attacks on shared enemies, or declarations of shared origins can be felt necessary to satisfy a wish for affiliation. Sometimes it simply corrupts the language, sometimes the meaning of the discourse.

I think anxiety about affiliation may be prevalent in psychoanalysis now, when greater movement between the sub-paradigmatic theoretical groupings (or schools of thought) is taking place. There seems to be uncertainty as to whether psychoanalytic theory is in a state of fragmentation or integration. If this is the case, one would expect more anxiety and conflict about publication with potentially more disguise or distortion within the text.

SUMMARY

I have suggested that publication anxiety is ubiquitous and natural; it can produce inhibition, symptomatic disorders of the text, or simply overt anxiety. Anxiety-free publication occurs where anxiety is denied as part of a manic defence which produces complacent orthodoxy, triumphant iconoclasm, or an illusion of originality. A discriminating journal usually detects this and publication fails.

If the anxiety is excessive, there may be an inhibition of publication such as afflicted Darwin. Lesser degrees of anxiety may result in distraction or distortion due to a compromise between the urge to communicate an idea and the desire to consolidate affiliation with a significant group through shared language, common belief systems, totemic figures or ritual utterances.

I see this conflict as internal to the individual. It is shaped by Oedipal anxieties which are given different emphasis and intensity by the scientific contexts current at the time. If the 'paradigm', under the influence of which the analyst is writing is in the ascendent, publication is relatively free of anxiety for most writers who are content to add to its application. Some, however, suffer 'anxiety of influence', fearing that their existence as originators of ideas is threatened. When the stability of the paradigm is threatened, due to the accumulation of anomalies, publication anxiety, with both persecutory and depressive elements is intensified. This increases the conflict between the need for affiliation and the desire for communication and may result in defensive writing or distorted texts.

Notes and Bibliography

Abraham K. (1924) 'A Short Study of the Development of the Libido, viewed in the light of the Mental Disorders' in *Selected Papers of Karl Abraham* trans. Douglas Bryan and Alix Strachey, Hogarth, London 1973

Abrams M. H. (1957) *A Glossary of Literary Terms* 4th Ed. Holt, Rhinehart and Winston, New York 1981

Bion W. R. (1962) 'Learning from Experience' Maresfield Reprints, Karnac, London 1984

.... (1963) 'Elements of Psycho-Analysis' Maresfield Reprints, Karnac, London 1984

.... (1970) 'Attention and Interpretation' Tavistock Publications, London

Bloom H. (1973) *The Anxiety of Influence* Oxford University Press

Britton R. (1983) 'Some Technical Difficulties in Speaking to the Patient' unpublished paper read in the British Psycho-Analytical Society

.... (1989) 'The Missing Link: Parental Sexuality in the Oedipus Complex' in *The Oedipus Complex Today* ed. J Steiner, Karnac Books, London

.... (1992) 'The Oedipus situation and the depressive position' in *Clinical Lectures on Klein and Bion* ed. R Anderson, Routledge: London and New York.

Desmond A. and Moore J. (1992) *Darwin* Penguin Books

Freud S. (1923a) 'A seventeenth century demonological neurosis' S.E. XIX pp69-108

.... (1923b) 'The infantile genital organisation: An interpolation into the theory of sexuality' S.E. XIX pp141-148

.... (1927) 'Humour' S.E. XXI pp159-166

.... (1933) 'The Question of a Weltanschauung' in *New Introductory Lectures on Psychoanalysis* S.E. XXII

Kuhn T. S. (1962) *The Structure of Scientific Revolutions* University of Chicago Press Ltd, Chicago

Rodman F. R. (1987) *The Spontaneous Gesture* Harvard University Press, Mass. and London

Ask me no questions and I'll tell you no lies - The social organization of secrets

Susan Budd

This paper considers some of the implications for psychoanalysis as a discipline which stem from the central role played by case material, as both its main source of evidence and as the medium for discussion and communication between its practitioners. When English psychoanalysts discuss their subject, they are usually not discussing theory but how to do it; how can particular events or emotions in an analytic session be understood, what are we to make of a particular sequence of sessions, how can we find our way through an apparent impasse, and so on. These questions arise out of working with specific cases, and to discuss them the analyst must provide us with detailed material. But there are many inherent difficulties in using and communicating case material in a way which allows for both proper understanding and detached reflection, and psychoanalysis has to develop both an etiquette and institutional arrangements which can allow this to happen.

The meaning of the first part of my title is that I think that we come to understand case material in a different way from the way that we understand the rest of psychoanalytic theory. We can only really understand it through a kind of intuitive identification with both the patient and the analyst, and this means that patients or other analysts can tell us her or his-stories, but if we want to understand them properly, at those times when they are working most creatively, at the limits of their understanding, we must listen carefully and not question them. Whilst often in a session or a seminar, to ask a question can be the obvious thing to do, or the best sort of interpretation, at these crucial times if we ask questions, we force the patient or therapist to lie or to falsify. This is not just because they feel they must keep something secret, or if they are the analyst, confidential, but because if they answer us, they answer in our terms, they give the material the shape that our question has implied rather than the shape which the material has for them, or which might have in due course emerged like one of those fabulous and unlikely creatures occasionally dredged up from the deep, whose nature we could not have previously envisaged or anticipated. 'The trouble with asking questions', my first analyst used to say, 'is that you get an answer.'

Although I hope that most practising psychotherapists will agree that this view, although exaggerated for rhetorical effect, contains at least some truth, obviously a shared discourse and discipline cannot be built up on such radical subjectivism. Facts cannot be understood without theories to organize them. To use theory, we have to be able to ask questions of each other; this has been clearly and cogently argued by David Tuckett, both at this conference and in the context of the editorial policy of the *International Journal of Psychoanalysis*.[1] For individuals, it is hard to publish, or even to report publicly, detailed clinical material, partly for the reasons that Ronald Britton describes in his paper in this volume. Some senior and well-respected analysts not only never publish, they never report on their clinical work in public; they feel that to do so is to betray the contract they have made with the patient. We must respect their decision, and their self-denial in not seeking for the support and approval of their peers, whilst recognizing that nonetheless, there is always a point at which concern for confidentiality, or respect for individuality, can become secrecy and a desire for concealment, or the solipsistic feeling that nobody can understand us anyway.

A discipline whose subject-matter is private and intimate, and concerned with secrets, is constrained in its organization. In particular it is problematic as to whether it can ever allow for the full and clear statement of case material which will let us decide whether the theory which was used to decipher the clinical facts was adequate or not. And yet, whatever we understand 'science' to be, being able to clearly and openly describe the data on which our hypotheses are based is a central part of it. If psychoanalysis is to have any claim to be a science, we have to find a way of communicating case material.

Clinical accounts are central to the routine practice of analysis or psychotherapy, because they are the medium by which we are trained and in which we demonstrate our competence, but they are also the method by which we ask questions, communicate new ideas to each other and convey a new understanding. Often case material can become a new nucleus, so to speak, around which various stray and random observations can gather to form a new category or perspective which may in turn become the basis for a new theory. In many disciplines, such as medicine or law, teaching centres round the idea of the case; it is here that theory is seen to be put into practice, and the student absorbs the rules, many of which are implicit, as to what he is looking for and how it is to be classified and treated. But in psychoanalysis, we cannot be present at the bedside or read depositions; we rely on the memory, knowing how fallible and selective our memory is, of one person who was present at a highly emotional encounter.

Perhaps we need to distinguish between the routine use of case material within the profession to report on our work to supervisors and in informal case presentations, and that where selected material is used in print to illustrate a point, and will be edited and presented accordingly. Case material tends to be produced for two purposes - to be read to a supervisor or seminar so that they can help us to process and understand it, or to be published or read on a more formal and public occasion, in order to support a theoretical argument or demonstrate a process. It is very rare to find a published record of relatively unselected material, partly because the process of recalling and recording sessions as fully as possible, as all students know too well, takes a great deal of effort and time. Melanie Klein, for example, said that she had only been able to record *The Narrative of a Child Analysis* because she was living in a remote part of Scotland during the war with little else to do; each session took her at least two hours to write up. Furthermore, after only a few weeks of recording such data, we must begin to select if we are not to drown, and yet the number of possible ways of selecting and understanding is multiplying fast; it is a truism amongst historians that generalisations are much easier where you don't have much evidence, and the sheer weight of raw data precludes understanding; we have to read it from a specific perspective.

In the early days of psychoanalysis, the problem of which perspective out of many to use so that we know what to report did not exist. Freud and his colleagues thought that clinical material would ultimately be organizable in terms of a general psychic pattern - this patient was orphaned early, or this one was excessively anally stimulated, and therefore the mental apparatus would have been affected in an ultimately predictable manner. They believed in psychic determinism, and therefore that they would be able to predict the kinds of character defences and unconscious fantasies which would result from specific early experiences or vicissitudes of instinct. Because Freud started off from a biological perspective on man he assumed that his theory was a universal one, which would apply to all human beings because they inhabit the same bodies and minds, and was not reliant on their particular understandings or circumstances.

But for reasons which are probably familiar to you, psychoanalysis, especially in Britain, has shifted toward seeing the individual in terms of a particular set of relationships or expectations which he or she tends to establish with all their important objects, especially, in the present, with the therapist. It is often said that every person, every analysis, is unique; and so they are, but we cannot escape from the fact that to describe them at all, we must use general terms. All thought, primary or secondary process, language itself, is based on the ability to classify and generalize. British Psychoanalysts have sometimes too readily skimmed over the many conceptual issues which are involved in making valid deductions from clinical material. (I was reminded by a member of the audience at the conference of M.L.J. Abercrombie's modest and illuminating study of how the perception and judgement of medical students was affected by pre-conscious factors[2].)

Psychoanalytic theory is of two types - general theories of

mental and emotional functioning, the diagnosis and aetiology of malfunctioning, the nature of unconscious processes, and so on, and a second kind, much more practical, which we might call the how-to-do-it level. What we read here is much more analogous to books which tell us how to do things: how someone built a house or hitch-hiked across Asia or was a successful sales manager. Other disciplines show the same division between theoretical knowledge and theories of practice, of how we actually put what we know into use when we are being practitioners.

There is a growing intellectual interest in psychoanalysis on the first level. In the United Kingdon, during the last few years there have been a growing number of university courses on psychoanalysis in its cultural context, in relation to feminism, literature, linguistics, film, and so on. Alongside this, however, psychoanalysis is also taught not only in public institutions but in privately-funded training organizations as a therapy, and as a technique. The students who study it here do so for a severely practical reason; they want to become psychoanalysts or psychoanalytically oriented psychotherapists, and so they want to know how to do it. To learn how to do it is very hard; the entities with which we deal are invisible and hard to identify and describe; the transference and counter-transference sway our perceptions and thoughts; and we are full of anxiety about whether we have got it right, whether we are causing unnecessary pain, and so on. So we are now more akin to apprentices than we are to the university students that we once were, and in this approach to learning about psychoanalysis the formative and transformative experiences will be to do with case material; our own analyses or therapies, our experiences with our supervisors, our training patients, and hearing our fellow-students discuss and present their work.

Many students will combine their engagement with the clinical with a continued interest in general psychoanalytic theory, but it is my impression that in most analytic trainings, especially in Britain, the crucial common denominator of the training, to which much anxiety is attached, is learning how to do it. Progress through trainings is assessed not by mastery of theory, but by progress in analysis and in supervision. Riccardo Steiner has repeatedly drawn our attention to the paradoxically strong influence of the British empiricist tradition on a group of European emigres. The English tradition is to assess knowledge in terms of how it works out in practice; P. S. Atiytah, for example, contrasts the English pragmatic legal tradition, where the authorities are judges and precendents, with the European and Scottish traditions, which are more concerned to be scientific and where academic jurists search for some degree of codification and logic[3]. The pragmatic attitude to law, he thinks, can lead to two opposing dangers; to a mindless and blind application of rules of thumb, or to an abandonment of rules.

> *By and large, English lawyers....have tended to think of it as almost a virtue to be illogical, and have ascribed that virtue freely to their law; 'being logical' is an eccentric continental practice, in which commonsensical Englishmen indulge at their peril.*[4]

Michael Rustin thinks that the peculiarly empiricist slant in British psychoanalysis, in which it is assumed that the theory will both emerge from and be confirmed by case material, may also be partly because many eminent British analysts were and are women, often seen as less interested or seduced than men are by general theoretical arguments.[5]

The cultural context plus the psychotherapy student's situation creates a particular slant in reading Freud and other classics, in which for the student, the case histories become the central texts. Students and their teachers return to the classical case-histories over and over again, but they read and understand them in ways which are different from the way in which a non-therapist does. A shift which I have repeatedly noticed whilst teaching, and which certainly was true of myself, is that non-therapists tend to understand case-histories by comparing themselves with the patient, whom they perceive both as victim and as essentially well, as if treatment was something which they could either take or let alone. They are therefore critical of anything which can be seen as jeopardizing the patient's autonomy. If they decide to become therapists, they begin to identify more with the analyst. At first, they can often be rather critical of both patient and analyst, as if anxious to show how much more they could see, or how much better they could do it. Later, they acquire a more realistic sense of how taxing psychoanalysis is to do, how uncertain and slow change is, and of how hard they need to work at preserving the autonomy of someone who may be severely regressed and would rather be dependent.

Both tendencies are especially marked in the readings of Dora, Freud's most frequently discussed and cited case. Non-therapists are not inclined to see Dora as really ill; she just suffered from being surrounded by sexual hypocrites and would have been better off if she and Freud had never met. Therapists are not inclined to see Dora in her historical context - in terms of the ideas that Freud was using at the time, or the other kinds of treatment that she might have had. (Modern commentators are inclined to see Freud as unable to listen to Dora; but at the start of the century Wilfrid Trotter, a promising young surgeon, having read *A Case of Hysteria*, remarked to his friend Ernest Jones that there was an interesting man in Vienna who actually listened to his patients).[6] Perhaps neither therapists nor intellectuals take seriously enough Freud's self-reflectiveness and self-doubts, which he expressed when he said that his case material read like a novel rather than a scientific treatise.

One implication of his remark was that he was moving towards a hermeneutic understanding of telling a case history. He was well-aware that he could have told the story differently, that different facts could have been selected, different emphases made, a different tone imparted to the text; he knew that when he wrote it his anger and frustration with Dora lent a particular clarity and brilliance to what he had to say. Although these changed emphases would not have changed the plot, they would have given a different meaning to the story. We may also guess that the drive behind the narrative of the case-history was the greater because the treatment was so short - it only lasted for three months. Had it continued, qualifications, other emphases, other ways of seeing the same material, other combinations of ideas would have occurred, Dora herself would have imperceptibly changed, and Freud would have been torn between a clear narrative thrust, and trying to represent simultaneously the alternative ways in which he could have presented and interpreted his material. As analyses have become much longer, in Britain we have chosen a different method of selection, by focusing on a single session or sessions looked at largely from the perspective of the shifting relationship between patient and analyst; but each session, however rich, cannot contain the truth of an analysis, any more than an analysis can contain the whole truth of a human life.

The distinction between general psychoanalytic theory and the theory contained in case-material is similar to the distinction between theories based on the general pattern of alternatives available at a moment in time - for example, the idea that the human sexual impulse can follow one of a number of alternative paths, or that we can evade and attack thinking in a number of classifiable ways - and an historical, or linear and causal account of a particular individual, of great depth and complexity, but seen in terms of his or herself, where no attempt is made to see how typical or atypical he or she is, whether and why other people show similar consequences from similar childhood events, and so on. It will be evident to those with a background in history or the social sciences that this is an old debate. Radcliffe-Browne, for instance, termed the two ways of seeing the nomothetic and the ideographic. Donald Spence makes a similar distinction in *The Rhetorical Voice of Psychoanalysis* (1994).[7]

He contrasts the Aristotelian, rhetorical conceptualist tradition, which tends to rely on the case-history, with the Galilean, empiricist, quantifying tradition, which relies on the accumulation and comparison of observations by a number of collaborators in order to test general hypotheses. He is strongly in favour of the latter, partly because he sees it as more scientific, democratic and less elitist - the former tradition, as he says, tends towards the assumption that some raconteurs are more gifted than others and that the truth is self-evident and intelligible through intuition alone, and this means that the ability of such gifted raconteurs to tell us case-histories convincingly, or to put interpretations to their patients in such a way that they will accept them, lies in their command of rhetoric.

It seems inevitable that this must be so in a clinical discipline such as psychoanalysis, where learning and expertise are passed on between individuals. Some psychoanalytic practitioners are or are seen as very much more gifted than others; that they attract supporters, who try to absorb and adopt their expertise by close association and by emulation, is not surprising. This is particularly likely to happen if it is thought that their views cannot be codified or summarized, ie. if they are nearer to the how-to-do-it end of the theoretical spectrum. Part of the appeal of the writings of certain psychoanalysts to the practitioner is that they were acknowledged to be outstanding clinicians; Melanie Klein and Donald Winnicott were, for example. We read the literature, as we search out supervisors, with the hope of finding insights which will help us understand our patients. Freud once confessed ruefully that he thought he was too impatient to be a good clinician; and this remark has been taken up and repeated in the teeth of aspects of several of his case-histories which to me suggest quite the reverse.

If part of what makes interpretations more acceptable is their form, or what Spence calls their 'narrative fit', if the demands of rhetoric affect the way that we put things, this seems unavoidable. It seems unlikely to me that we could ever hear interpretations and submit them to some kind of rational testing or scrutiny before deciding to accept or reject them - rather, they seem to feel 'right' or 'wrong', or to proceed from someone who feels empathic, or angry, or distant - ie. our subjective sense of feeling understood or not comes into play. The assumption that we can speak directly to the patient's unconscious has always seemed to me to be rather unlikely; of its nature, the unconscious seems not able to hear very well. This view must be strengthened by the research on early child-parent interaction, where we can see more and more clearly that the general mood, timing, rhythm and so on of mother and child's behaviour is crucially important to the responsiveness of each to the other. We now attach more weight to the general form and mood of the session as distinct from its content than we did; and yet our observation of this is more likely to be subjective and fallible. The hope that we can firmly separate fact and fiction, or theory and observation, and move away from the subjective element in understanding, so that we do not use analogies and argue directly from the evidence, seems to me to be unlikely to be realisable.

The current situation in psychoanalysis seems akin to that in history and anthropology, where it has increasingly been felt that each epoch has its own criteria of intelligibility; that if we are to understand why what happened happened, we have to start from the subjective understanding of people at the time.[8] To think that twins are birds, or that to dream of having sex with your mother-in-law means the crops will fail, or that the glance of menstruating women turns milk sour, are beliefs which cannot be wrenched from their context if we are to understand them. We can understand why people have these particular beliefs; we can even understand why within their terms they find certain things puzzling, or make errors, but we can only do so by trying to understand their minds and social context as a whole.[9] And one of the rewards of making the effort to do so is that by implication it forces us to see ourselves more from the outside. The analogies with the development of interest in the counter-transference in psychoanalysis seem clear; as we begin to see how complex and intricate our mutual understanding is, the otherness of the other person throws into relief the otherness of ourselves and the need to scrutinize our own judgement.

In the last decade or so, many historians have moved on yet further into a more radical subjectivity. They no longer try to produce a general account of a social change like the rise of the welfare state, or falling family-size, but rather an account of a particular group or individual's perspective on such an event, accepting that we have only a multiplicity of perspectives, none of which can be said to be wholly true or false. Above all, as we add to our understanding, the situation subtly changes; we never step into the same river twice, said Heraclitus, the first historian. Thinking inside psychoanalysis is affected by general intellectual shifts; our notion of a good theory, or more concretely, to take a recent controversial example, as to whether homosexuality is to be understood as a perversion or not, is deeply affected by general societal change, and our increasing sensitivity as to whose account it is anyway must be related to the growing awareness of the issue of mentalities in other disciplines.

The situation in which a situation can be understood in terms of general theories until we approach nearer to how-to-do-it, to putting that general knowledge and perspective into operation in the world at which point we begin to use heuristic knowledge, is quite common. Perhaps the nearer we approach to postgraduate studies, knowledge at the point of use - this is similar to what Thomas Kuhn was saying - the more we rely on the kind of knowledge which is described by phrases such as case law, rules of thumb, clinical intuition, listening to the feel of music, green fingers for the economy, the inner game of tennis, and so on. The earliest stages of any field of knowledge are likely to be fully codified and accepted, but as we try to put that knowledge to use in the real world, then the interface between that which we carry in our heads and try to apply, and the external world which often responds unpredictably to our efforts, becomes more uncertain. We may know the rules of tort, or the changes in tissue histology produced by various kinds of cancer, or the nature of projective identification, but the application of this technical knowledge to a particular person at a particular time is always more uncertain. This is because such knowledge is bound up with our own subjectivity - not only of our observations and judgements, but those of the person we are dealing with.

For a long time from the 1960's onward, in psychoanalysis as in other fields, those practitioners who were concerned with the methodological status of what they were doing (often bound up with the question, 'Is it a Science?') were greatly influenced by both Karl Popper, who tended to aggregate all properly scientific knowledge to what he believed to be the methodology of physics, to him the queen of the sciences, and by Thomas Kuhn, with his rather more flexible and historically plausible view of progress in science, the concept of the growth of dominant paradigms and their eventual modification, and the consequent splitting of fields of enquiry. Both these writers briefly discussed psychoanalysis, but whilst conceeding the interest of its subject matter were inclined to reject it as unscientific and unproven. There are other writers on the nature of scientific knowledge, less well-known, whom I have found more illuminating in thinking about what kind of knowledge we use in clinical work.

The first is Herbert Simon, one of the founders of the study of artificial intelligence, who published a little-known book called *The Sciences of the Artificial.*[10] Amongst the sciences of the manmade or artificial, he included economics, engineering, and psychology, to which we might add psychoanalysis. They are located at the interface between the given world which is external to men, which can be studied by the natural sciences, and the micro-world inside us, of physiology, biochemistry and so on, equally susceptible to positivist analysis. But in the middle are the sciences which study artificial structures or systems which men have created, which are shot through with subjectivity, with human goals and purposes, with men's mutual understanding and self-awareness. They are concerned with artifacts, and how they function in different environments, and therefore not only with what is but what ought to be, and how it can be brought about. And yet despite this, they have internal criteria of what is and what is not a reasonable or truthful statement. The law, for example, is clearly not a science; but it is an orderly body of knowledge, to which we can bring evidence to show how well it functions in regulating the social world.

Simon observes that the term 'artificial' has pejorative associations which are built into language itself. It is as though by admitting that we have made something rather than having discovered it, we find it not just non-natural but unnatural, and spurious. In psychoanalysis, I think that we can react to the artifice of case-histories, ie. to the self-evident selection of both what is presented and to the particular way that the analyst decided to react in the session, as if it was very disturbing. The attempts to codify and standardize reporting and technique are partly due to the longing for a more absolute, 'natural' knowledge which could make us feel safer in what we do.

I return to the question of how we learn to do analysis in the first place, and the role of clinical material as the crucial factor in creating our understanding of what psychoanalysis is. This has echoes in some of the work by historians of science which focuses on the importance of learning technique in forming a concept of what their science is. For example, J.R. Ravetz[11] discusses how scientists actually learn to do research, and the actual conditions under which good research can be done. He argues that science is what scientists do; they acquire their sense of what they are looking for, of what is valuable and what is not, of the point of what they are doing, by learning technique. They become scientists by learning how to do science, and like the rest of us, they learn by being apprentices. In being taught how to do science, without realizing it they imbibe the general perspectives of those that they learn from.

In the same way, when students think that they are learning about psychoanalysis just because they want to learn how to do it, how to become analysts or psychotherapists, I think that they are also imbibing, without realizing it, theories about the nature of psychoanalysis itself. The empiricist's position, that you can just read case material and know how to assess it and what it means, or sit in a session and know what to say, doesn't hold water; the invisible hand of theory is conditioning us in what to notice and how to interpret it. Students learn by trial and error what kind of case material it is appropriate to present; what should be mentioned, what can be left out.

If we read case-histories from different periods, or from different analytic schools, we notice different emphases. More or less of the patient's history is included; it is assumed to be more or less objectively true or distorted by instinct and transference; different kinds of traumatic events are included in the account. Few accounts now, for example, would include whether a patient had been breast-fed or not; but there would probably be careful attention to the ages of siblings or the possibility of sexual abuse. Similarly, the interpretations which are given direct the patient's attention to areas which are thought to be important by the analyst; patients who have had more than one therapist are well-aware of this, and can see how what the analyst saw as important was due in part to their personality and to the kind of analysis that they had had, as well as whatever theoretical views they came to form. (I don't want to over-emphasize the extent to which we are dominated by our analyses; there is a tendency in the therapeutic milieu, I think, to see students as created by their training-analyses, rising like phoenixes reborn from the ashes of their old identities. This view seems insulting to the creativity of both student and training-analyst, and also idealizes the power of the analytic process to radically transform our personalities, to cut us free from what our parents and early histories made of us.)

For example, psychotherapy students in England at the moment are likely to notice that their supervisors discuss with them breaks or interruptions in treatment and encourage them to interpret them; in presenting case-material, their peers will probably include accounts of their counter-transference, or if they don't, the seminar-leader or supervisor is likely to ask them about it. These emphases are not just random; they proceed from views about the nature of mother-baby interaction which are part of the dominant English perspective, but the student may well not be aware of this; he or she just knows that this is the sort of material which should be systematically noticed and reported. This factor, the learning what we are supposed to look for, is the main thing which determines all our learning and understanding in any science, any discipline.

In psychoanalysis, we are constrained in what we can report or publish about patients by requirements of confidentiality, of secrecy. This is one reason for the continued popularity in discussions of the classical case-histories; the damage has already been done, and done at a time when sensitivity about how patients might feel about what was said seems to have been less. It also accounts for the use of case-discussions based on fictional characters, where despite their obvious limitations, no harm can be done. Obviously, the requirements of confidentiality vary from audience to audience, from large public meetings to a private consultation between colleagues. As many analyses are conducted with patients who are future colleagues, or are related to colleagues, or have contacts with the therapeutic milieu, or are generally well-read professional people who will probably be curious enough about their analyst to read what he has written, the problem is compounded.

An additional problem is that although for us, the discussion of case-material is relatively routine, outside the therapeutic milieu it has all the glamour and excitement of the secret, and some rather odd things tend to happen in meetings where case material is presented to a lay audience. Very often a member of the audience will unwittingly identify strongly with some aspect of the person being presented, and react as if they are being attacked; others may then react by analyzing their reactions, and Freud's warnings of the dangers of wild analysis are all too vividly borne out.

Because of changes in the wider world, psychoanalysts are becoming more and more sensitive to issues of confidentiality, and tailoring their case-presentations accordingly. It is now quite rare in Britain for much material to be presented which is about the history proper of the patient; what we get is the detailed report of a session, in which we consider in detail the mental functioning of someone anonymous. The trouble is, I think, that because this is all we easily can present, we slide imperceptibly to the view that this is all that we should present, everything that it is important to know about the patient in order to understand him. And this, I think, may be one of the reasons why we no longer stress the importance of the patient's history, but assume that everything that we need to know will become evident in the transference. This belief is highly convenient. But what is being eroded all the time is the kind of material which makes case-histories, and analyses, comparable; which makes it possible to assess comparatively the relationship between history and pathology, the effectiveness of particular kinds of interpretation, all the data that we need in order to make some kind of claim for analysis as a discipline where causal links can be assessed and weighed.

Donald Spence and David Tuckett are both deeply concerned about this, and want to urge upon us the necessity for writing about patients in terms of 'thick description' - Spence's term - ie. in a way which makes objective comparison and assessment possible. I agree with their anxieties and with their concern that we should not allow criteria of proof and testing in psychoanalysis to go by the board. But can we combine the increasing practical necessity of confidentiality, and the inherently solipsistic nature of each analysis, with the constraint to produce objectively assessable material ?

Bibliography and notes

1. D. Tuckett (1995) 'The Conceptualization and Communication of Clinical Facts in Psychoanalysis' *International Journal of Psycho-Analysis*, Vol. 76(4): 653-62

2. M.L.J. Abercrombie (1989) *The Anatomy of Judgement - An Investigation into the Processes of Perception and Reasoning* Free Association Books (first published in 1960).

3. P.S.Atiyah (1987) *Pragmatism and Theory in English Law, 39th Hamlyn Lectures* Stevens.

4. MacCormick, Regius Professor of Public Law at Edinburgh, quoted in Atiyah, op cit., pp.9-10.

5. See, for example, Riccardo Steiner (1991) 'Some Thoughts about tradition and change arising from the British Psycho-Analytical Society's Controversial Discussions, 1943-44,' *International Review of Psychoanalysis* Vol.12 (1), 1985, pp.27-71; and Michael Rustin, 'The Social Organization of Secrets' in *The Good Society and the Inner World- Psychoanalysis, Politics and Culture* Verso, London.

6. Ernest Jones (1990) *Free Associations* Transaction Publishers, London, pp.149-50.

7. Donald P. Spence (1994) 'Retreat from Galileo', in *The Rhetorical Voice of Psychoanalysis: Displacement of Evidence by Theory* Harvard University Press.

8. Many of the relevant papers are to be found in *Rationality* (1970) edited by B.R. Wilson, Blackwell.

9. Early psychoanalytic commentators on society tended to go wrong at this point; they wrote as if a particular symbol or belief had a constant social meaning, and as if personality could be assessed in the same way regardless of cultural context. Similarly, social scientists have tended to misunderstand and over-simplify psychoanalysis, taking the Oedipus Complex, for example, to be an account of how the child related to and incorporated an actual mother and father, ignoring the implications of Freud's statement that we identify with both parents both actively and passively, as well as the more recent tendency to see the oedipal conflict as being about the difficulty in tolerating a third person, or being out of control in our relationships and our thinking. Perhaps all practitioners, understandably, tend towards reductionist and out-of-date versions of other disciplines.

10. H.A.Simon (1969) *The Sciences of the Artificial - Karl Taylor Compton Lectures* The M.I.T. Press.

11. J.R.Ravetz (1971) *Scientific Knowledge and its Social Problems* Oxford University Press.

Case histories and the institutionalisation of psychoanalysis

Julia Borossa

Let us start with two quotations. The first one, appropriately, is from Freud himself, writing to his close friend and collaborator, Sandor Ferenczi on the 8th of May 1913:

> *We should brace ourselves for the collapse of the organization at the Congress. Of course, everything that strives to get away from our truths has public approval in its favor. It is quite possible that they will really bury us this time....*[1]

The second quotation is considerably more recent. Joan Copjec, in introducing a new book series by the publishers Verso, writes:

> *the series - recognizing the precarious status of psychoanalysis in our contemporary world, wants to reaffirm the critical power of Freudian theory.* [2]

Psychoanalysis is precarious. This common theme readily emerges despite the span of almost a century separating the two remarks, despite the wildly different contexts in which they were uttered: the beleaguered early psychoanalytic movement and contemporary academia, respectively. Consequently, I am moved to speculate that this precariousness might well be structural, as well as historical. One could well unearth dozens, perhaps even hundreds of similar statements, marking the path of the development of the discipline throughout the twentieth century. Psychoanalysis, then, whether it is defined as a theory, a body of knowledge, or as a set of practices and social organisations, (and my contention is that it must be *all* of these), is precarious. The aim of this essay is to explore some of the conceptual and institutional reasons which underlie this precariousness. Its main thesis is that the special place that the clinical encounter holds in psychoanalysis is intrinsic to its precariousness.

In the introduction to a recent collection of essays, edited by Mark Micale and Roy Porter, *Discovering the History of Psychiatry*, psychiatry is presented as 'poised precariously between the medical sciences and the human sciences' and its distinctive historical structure is described as 'scattered in a multitude of areas of past activity and inquiry, including primitive medicine, mythology, hypnotism, theology, philosophy, law, anthropology, literature, and popular lay healing'.[3] Psychiatry itself, therefore, is not presented as a stable, self-contained field of inquiry, but rather as one which gains its identity in relation to these neighbouring fields, and changes its characteristics as these fields expand or contract. Psychoanalysis is rightly represented in the collection I am referring to, as one 'inflection' of psychiatry, inasmuch as it shares precisely the multifaceted historical structure described in the quotation. But does it follow that the domain of medicine is a stable one, in contrast? Or is it not just as much in flux, as our understanding of the body, and its connection to the psyche shifts and the interaction between its practitioners, doctors and patients alters, as the nature of the discipline changes over time and over cultures? These are fundamental questions which must be borne in mind.

It is impossible to consider the emergence of psychoanalysis as a discipline in its own right, without accounting for the nature of the circulation and distribution of knowledge between the patient and the one who heals. In this respect, in psychoanalysis, the textual genre of the case history is sure to have a key, albeit paradoxical, status and role. Clinical writing is simultaneously called to function as a narrative representation of the *private interaction* between patient and analyst and as a regulator of psychoanalysis as a discipline and an institution, therefore very much part of the *public domain*. In considering this paradox, a meditation on the relationship between psychoanalysis as a discipline, and history as a discipline, and on the ways in which the roles and preoccupations of the psychoanalyst and the historian might or might not interact and inform one another, proves illuminating.

I wish to invoke three theoretical starting points, and 'takes' on the matter. The first is an essay by Arnold Davidson, with the very apt title 'How to do the History of Psychoanalysis?' which engages explicitly with Michel Foucault's influence on historiography.[4] The second is a book by the historian of psychoanalysis Elisabeth Roudinesco, *Genealogies*,[5] which bears in its title an implicit homage to Foucault's method of historical enquiry. Starting as an account of her personal history, the book merges into an account of how the author found her voice as historian, and finally into that historian's own theory of how to write the history of psychoanalysis. The third reference point is a recent book by Jacques Derrida, *Mal d'archives*, based on a lecture he gave in 1994 at a Freud Museum conference, 'Memory: the Question of Archives'. The ambiguity of the French 'mal' is inadequately rendered in either of the possible English translations, 'the ache of archives', or 'the evil of archives'.[6] The text itself addresses precisely a kind of missed encounter between the historian and the psychoanalyst, crystallized in the idea of the archive, which has definite implications for both history and psychoanalysis.

Arnold Davidson's essay is a fitting point of departure for the discussion, because it invokes, following Foucault's archaeological method, the idea of the conceptual break, and of a history of concepts dependent on the circumstances in which they become intelligible. Comparing Freud's ideas on perversion as expressed in the *Three Essays on Sexuality* with other sexological texts of the period, Davidson shows ways in which Freud's writings provided a conceptual framework for emerging ways of thinking, and therefore a means for indelibly influencing our thought. As Auden put it in his poetic homage to Freud: 'To us he is no more a person than a whole climate of opinion'. Auden's words were suggestive of a Freud who was, as Foucault aptly phrased it, a 'founder of discursivity', and raise, I think the paradox of 'singularity'. Who is Freud, then, but the starting point of any history of psychoanalysis? His case histories, all his cherished writings, are touchstones we keep returning to.

In *Genealogies,* Elisabeth Roudinesco addresses also the paradox of singularity, and does so from the point of view of the historian. The form of the book, one which, she explains in the introduction, had already been adopted by the historian Philippe Ariès, and then in a collective work, by Maurice Agulhon, Jacques Le Goff and others, has been called an *'ego-histoire'*. Its method is described as one that proposes to 'shed light on one's own history, rendering explicit the link between the history one writes and that which has written one'.[7] The resonances with analysis and self-analysis are certainly there, as well as the paradox inherent in the task. As Roudinesco puts it:

> *I am not haunted by the mystery of time, but that of exile, of loss, of the archive. The passage to the identity of historian is a desire for transcendence, for a return to the origins marked by the traces of a becoming: the history of a family history. In the mise-en-scene of our family tree, when the ego is no longer master in its own house, the notion of identity is no longer one that holds.*[8]

The paradox reaches its crises point, its enactment, at the moment when the author recounts herself as starting to write a history of psychoanalysis which she has literally witnessed. It is Derrida, a philosopher who has so long been preoccupied with questions of signature and authorship, who is portrayed in the text as pointing this out to her. He asks: 'are you going to make use of the first person singular?'[9] This constitutes a key moment in the text, in which the historian's authority is challenged by the irruption of a singularity which is, I would argue, something that the psychoanalyst must always contend with.

Derrida's own discussion of the historian's task is laid out in the text I mentioned, *Mal d'archives*. The archive, for him is a space which preserves, but is predicated by the very idea of destruction. Quite simply, there would be no archive without the possibility of forgetting. Derrida, engages with the historian, keeper and engineer of the archive, or rather a particular historian, Joseph Hayim Yerushalmi, historian of Judaism, author of the book *Freud's Moses*.[10] That latter text is subjected to a close reading in order to arrive at a critique of the historian's privilege, which Derrida perceives as tantamount to loading the dice, as it were, in order to collapse the tension of preserving / destroying, thereby privileging a historical singularity, under the guise of a claim to the absolute.

The most dramatic moment in both Yerushalmi's text, and Derrida's critique, occurs in a section of *Freud's Moses* entitled 'Monologue with Freud'. Yerushalmi calls the spectre of Freud as witness in order that he may confirm the historian's reconstruction of psychoanalysis as Jewish science, and then promises that spectre not to reveal its secret answer. What scandalous behavior for a historian, to keep secrets, Derrida intones, but is it not just what is expected from the psychoanalyst? In other words, the argument hinges on the question of keeping / telling, and closely allied with this, is the issue of authorisation.

A science of archive must include a theory of its institutionalisation, in other words of the law that begins to be inscribed within it and of the right that authorises it. This right poses or supposes a network of boundaries which have their history, one that could be deconstructed. Psychoanalysis would not have been a stranger to this deconstruction.[11]

It would seem that the missed encounter between psychoanalysis and history hinges on the issue of representation. Taken in both senses, the artistic or narrative sense and the political one. I would like to argue at this point that one way of approaching the dialectic of history and psychoanalysis, to understand what is at stake in the network of boundaries that unifies and separates them, is through the 'ineffable' of the clinical encounter, and the ways in which that encounter could or could not be represented. A history of psychoanalysis then becomes possible through the archival traces of its practice, in other words, through the various narratives of the clinical encounter. Such a history would be at a point of tension between singular and the general, the private and the public.

A speculation about the nature of the psychoanalytic case history, the text which remains as the official record of the clinical relationship when the flow of speech between analyst and analysand has stopped, implies quite a fundamental speculation about the nature and the limits of psychoanalytic knowledge itself. Psychoanalysis is a discipline which sets itself up simultaneously as a way of curing and a particular form of knowing. Functioning as a record of the relationship between patient and therapist, as a proving ground for theoretical issues, as well as a teaching tool, the case history as text intimately entwines the practice, the epistemology and the institution of psychoanalysis, and grounds the discipline as an endeavor which functions simultaneously as a form of knowing and as a way of curing.

But how? Under what conditions?

Disciplines of the mind, as well as disciplines of the body, psychiatry, psychoanalysis, medicine, obviously exist within the changing social and cultural contexts which frame an equally changing relationship between patients and practitioners. But undoubtedly, the patient/analyst relationship which finds its way into clinical accounts, does so in a very particular *institutional* context. That institutional context is particular because it both contains and somehow does violence to the singularity of psychoanalysis. To institutionalise is to create rules, provide a stable, containing framework. And how can you do that with something as fundamentally unstable as psychoanalysis, the science of the unconscious, the cure through the clinical encounter?

On the 11th of April 1907, Jung was entering the golden phase of his involvement with Freud and with psychoanalysis. He had visited the professor in Vienna for the first time a month previously and he wrote him the following lines:

> *With your help I have come to see pretty deeply into things, but I am still far from seeing them* clearly. *Nevertheless I have the feeling of having made considerable inner progress since I got to know you personally; it seems to me that one can never quite understand your science unless one knows you in the flesh. Where so much still remains dark to us outsiders only faith can help; but the best and most effective faith is knowledge of your personality.*[12]

Jung's remarks touch upon the important paradox at the heart of any attempt to systematise psychoanalytic knowledge. As the subject of the unconscious that any adherent to psychoanalysis must deem himself or herself to be, seeing deeply does not necessarily lead one to a clear or complete picture. Moreover, self-analysis in this configuration is *a priori* impossible and this would imply that something additional was necessary in the pursuit of psychoanalytic (self) knowledge.

In this passage, Jung is positing Freud himself, or rather, the disciple's access to Freud, as the only sure guide, the one conceivable point of entry to whatever psychoanalytic knowledge there was to be had. It is possible to extrapolate from here: enlightenment is to be found in the psychoanalytic relationship itself. In this example, the relationship between Freud and Jung is, granted, only informally analytic, nevertheless their relationship, as it affects Jung's capacity to reminisce, retains the essential structural aspects of the one between patient and analyst. But already there was not enough of Freud to go around. After the initial years of informal meetings and discussions among a smallish and close-knit group, Freud's work was becoming increasingly known. As more and more interested parties were joining the movement, it was no longer possible to proceed in an *ad hoc* manner. It therefore became imperative to find the appropriate way to transmit the 'Freud factor'.[13]

A few years into his relationship with Jung, in one of the programmatic papers on technique that he wrote in the early years of the psychoanalytic movement, Freud first explicitly endorsed the idea of a systematic schooling for psychoanalysts.[14] He advocated an informal method of training, quasi-interchangeable with the patient/analyst interaction. This early model of psychoanalytic instruction would remain as an ideal, undercutting and jarring with the formal institutional framework which would soon be set up around it. A question insists and resonates throughout the history of psychoanalytic institutions: what relation does a training analysis have to just plain, analysis? A compelling belief in the power of 'authentic experience' (the experience of analysis, first and foremost) permeated Freud's initial wish to find formal ways of transmitting psychoanalysis, a wish which matched the desire of early colleagues such as Jung. As Freud's wish was translated into recommendations and eventually rules, institutional realities were found to fall short of the quasi-imponderable investment in the 'experiential' as a means of transmitting psychoanalytic knowledge.[15] In this context the question of rules and formal structures appeared problematic from the outset. In other words: how does one institutionalise psychoanalysis, when so much of it rests on imponderables such as 'the experience of analysis'. A surge in the popularity of psychoanalysis[16], which was soon followed by the first of many controversies and splits, namely Freud's break with

Jung, a crisis which also provides the context to Freud's apocalyptic remark which opens this paper. Therefore, it made good administrative as well as good pedagogic sense to actually formalise the recommendation that all prospective analysts undergo analysis as part of their analytic instruction.

The Berlin Psychoanalytic Institute dedicated to the training of new analysts opened in March 1920.[17] This Institute developed a three part curriculum consisting of a personal analysis, supervisions and lectures / seminars which remains the basis of the psychoanalytic training system to this day. The latter component, lectures / seminars is fairly unproblematic. As for the other two, their very nature (the privacy and particularity involved), jars with the idea of institutionalisation and raised and still raise all kinds of questions.

I will concentrate on the component of supervised analysis, which stood within the Berlin curriculum, midway between the other two components, the theoretical and the experiential. It was introduced a few years after teaching got under way at the Berlin Institute and was essentially a formalisation of an unofficial network of consultation which had operated among analysts until that point in time. Therese Benedek recalled the early days:

> *My first case was a self-referral. He probably had read more psychoanalysis than I had at that time. (...) My second case, referred by a local physician, was very puzzling and I sought help from Eitingon, whom I saw irregularly sometimes in Berlin and sometimes in Leipzig in his parents' home.*[18]

It is not only the informality of the way that Benedek learned her craft that is striking in this account, but the confusion of the patient / analyst / teacher roles which she hints at.

Members of the Hungarian Psychoanalytic Society sought to both clarify and make use of this aspect of supervision in their particular conception of analytic training. Starting with *Developments in Psychoanalysis*, a little book which Sandor Ferenczi co-wrote with Otto Rank,[19] Hungarian analysts argued for a model of supervision which accepted its close relationship to analysis, and was dedicated above all to solving problems which remained unresolved in the trainees' proper analysis and were therefore in danger of overflowing into a different, professional space. Vilma Kovacs, in an influential paper 'Training and Control analysis' explicitly raised the issue of the danger involved in unresolved countertransference, and the inadequate skills of the trainee. When does it become 'right to entrust patients to a candidate?', she asks.[20] In posing that question, Kovacs explicitly problematises the moment of the analysand's entry into his or her role as analyst. It followed that the Budapest school proceeded to institutionalise the affinity they saw between analysis and supervision and stipulated that the trainee's supervisor on his or her first case would be their analyst. Ultimately, these early difficulties over the formulation of an adequate training system touched on the limits of analysability. What constitutes analysis? Who is qualified to practice it? Is it possible to separate it from other activities? How can this newly professionalised discipline define its goals and its limitations?

'Analysis Terminable and Interminable' was a text of Freud's old age and it can be seen to constitute Freud's explicit answer to Ferenczi and the Hungarian School. The Professor had fought, and if not entirely won his battles, the future of psychoanalysis was nevertheless reasonably secure. And so he openly reflected upon a tragic paradox in his life's work: psychoanalysis was the 'impossible profession', a profession in which, as in education and government definite results always proved elusive.[21] The 'impossible profession' is a highly evocative phrase[22] and it points to a real paradox at the very heart of psychoanalysis taken as a body of knowledge to be systematised and institutionalised. Furthermore, he saw no guarantee that the benefits of analysis could be retained. In 'Analysis Terminable and Interminable', he went as far as suggesting that analysts should return to the couch regularly. It is significant that in that paper, Freud discusses on an equal footing three of his analytic relationships, all unfinished, all flawed. Freud identifies one of them as his famous patient the Wolf-Man, with whom he admitted to experimenting with ways of accelerating the treatment and ultimately failing him.[23] The other two cases involve a woman and a man whom Jones would identify as Ferenczi. If in this late pessimistic text Freud is finding the achievements of psychoanalytic therapy insubstantial and the profession of psychoanalysis 'impossible', he is explicitly questioning the very possibility of institutionalising psychoanalysis. It is fitting that in his account, the division of roles that institutionalisation imposes no longer holds. In a situation where a training analysis is something to be undergone every five years, all analysts stay patients for life. It is precisely this closeness between the identity of the analyst and the identity of the patient, which we have seen institutionalised in the idea of supervised analysis, that now returns as a threat undermining the profession of psychoanalysis.

From his early papers on technique to 'Analysis Terminable and Interminable', Freud conducted an ongoing reflection on whether it was possible to institutionalise psychoanalysis. I wish to go on to argue that Freud's clinical writings, the case histories that he wrote in the formative years of the profession of psychoanalysis, allowed for an alternate space to confront this problem. Moreover, his disciples made use of these texts in order to speculate about the nature of their work and their status as practitioners. This discussion will concentrate on the penultimate case that Freud published, the work entitled 'From the History of an Infantile Neurosis', otherwise known as the Wolf-Man case, which, as a recent critic put it 'seems to have been Freud's test case for the establishment of psychoanalysis as a transmissible school of thought'.[24]

The Wolf-Man case, is closely linked to the first serious upheavals of the psychoanalytic movement. Although published in 1918, Freud in fact wrote the text four years earlier. He explicitly stated in his very first footnote that the case history was conceived to discredit the work of the wayward disciples Jung and Adler.[25] Freud needed a powerful retort to Jung's virtual denial of infantile sexuality. The Wolf-Man case constituted such a retort: it is widely acknowledged to be a masterful narrative feat by Freud, revolving around an exploration of the primal scene, and its relationship to a child's sexuality. 'Whatever else the Jung affair produced, it helped to define publicly what Freud thought psychoanalysis really stood for'.[26]

'Did the child see? What did he see?' stand as the explicit and urgent questions of Freud's narrative. But most significantly, a third question, an implicit one, informs and frames the other two. 'How can I tell the story?' is Freud's recurrent question as he tries to solve once and for all the riddle of the primal scene as actual memory and / or retrospective construction. Freud's narrative task is a formidable one: as leader of the psychoanalytic movement, the guardian of 'his invention' psychoanalysis, he must have proof positive of the primacy of infantile sexuality. On the other hand, the nature of the interaction between patient and analyst prevent

Freud from giving his own answers to his first two questions. The answers had to be provided at the pace set by the unconscious, attain the degree of plenitude that the unconscious allowed, yet they had to be absolutely persuasive. How indeed could he tell the story?

Freud's strategy was to accentuate the complexity of the narrative. The answer may well lie, as in his other cases, in the power of the Oedipus complex, but the case would have to try to do justice to the circumcuitous road that would lead the patient there. Freud states this clearly: 'I am unable to give either a purely historical or a purely thematic account of my patient's story; I can write a history neither of the treatment nor of the illness'.[27] Freud gives us a series of intricately arranged stories: accounts of the patient as a child, of the various people who interacted with him, of his physical surroundings, of the fairy tales and family legends that served as a backdrop to his psychic world. The famous nightmare of the still white wolves is told late, almost mid-way into the text. Other stories follow it, stories already familiar to the analyst concerning the effects produced by either witnessing or fantasising about parental intercourse, intersected with partial accounts of the event itself.

Freud leaves the matter of the primal scene open for most of the text, providing the 'solution' in the penultimate section of the case study, and then proceeding to follow up this 'solution' with a concluding section entitled 'recapitulations and problems', opening up a path towards further psychoanalytic inquiry.

In a different institutional context, that of Anglo-American literary criticism, Freud's text has invited two diametrically opposed readings, both concerned with Freud's narrative technique. Peter Brooks [28] discusses the Wolf-Man case as a masterpiece of open-ended discourse, praising Freud's capacity to incorporate a tolerance for incertitude into his prose. Although initially comparing the genre of the case history to that most contrived narrative genre of detective fiction, Brooks argues that Freud is pushed by his patient's refusal to comply with his explanations into uncharted territory. Both patient and analyst are thus incapable of giving a straightforward, logical, reasonable narrative of events. Therefore, the Wolf-Man case through its constant problematisation of the ordering of events and through its refusal to decide on the status of the primal scene recognises that 'narrative sequences and scenarios must accord with the complex, twisting, subversive patternings of desire'.[29] Brooks concludes that 'like the modernist novel, the case history of the Wolf-Man shows up the limits of story-telling while nonetheless insisting that the story must get told'.[30]

In radically contrasting terms, Stanley Fish[31] attacks Freud's text for what he perceives to be its excessively tightly-knit rhetorical strategy. In other words, according to Fish, Freud never wondered how he could and would tell the story: he knew all along. In this view of the Wolf-Man case, the author uses tolerance for incertitude as a ploy which leaves neither the patient nor the reader any room to manoeuvre. 'The real story of the case is the story of persuasion, and we will be able to read it only when we tear our eyes away from the supposedly deeper story of the boy who had a dream'.[32] In Fish's view, Freud begins with the *assumption* of the primal scene, and cunningly uses this hypothesis as his evidence,[33] enjoying the 'pleasure of total mastery', heightening it 'by placing it in apparent jeopardy'.[34]

It is not the object of this discussion to argue the merits of Brooks' versus Fish's interpretation (or vice-versa), only to point to the very different conclusions they draw from their reading of Freud's text, a dialogic open-endedness on the one hand, a cunning authoritarianism on the other. This contrast makes sense if the case history is seen to be informed by additional questions which highlights its institutional status. Who is Freud telling the story to? Why is he telling it? The latter question has already been addressed: Freud is telling it to counter the views of Jung and Adler. As to whom Freud is telling the story, as in the case of all case histories, he is telling it first and foremost to his colleagues, to secure the continued expansion of a psychoanalytic establishment. At the start of the Wolf-Man case Freud had stated that his written account would of necessity fall short of the conviction bestowed by the practice of analysis itself: his account will be for the initiated, those who have already been convinced.[35] Whilst this is to a certain extent disingenuous (Freud certainly had much more at stake than preaching to the converted), it is also to be taken seriously. This case history, as well as all the others, were rallying points for the community of psychoanalysts, yardsticks against which they could measure their own work. Soon Freud's clinical writings would be on the curriculum of the new Institutes of psychoanalysis. They would be discussed by successive generations of analytic commentators.[36] I would like to suggest that rather than on the reader or the critic (be that critic a literary or psychoanalytic theorist), it is upon the practicing psychoanalyst, on the working disciple who dares to write, that a form of closure is imposed.

The Wolf-Man's second analyst was Ruth Mack Brunswick, a young American psychiatrist who came to Vienna to be analysed by Freud and quickly became an close family friend of Freud's, as well as his trusted disciple.[37] It was a mark of Freud's appreciation of her gifts as a clinician that in 1926, he referred to her the man who was clearly his prize patient. The Wolf-Man was then suffering from a near psychotic break-down which centered around a supposed blemish on his nose. According to him, an allegedly incompetent physician had operated on his nose, made matters worse, 'scarring him for life'. None of this was apparent to anybody else but he spent his days obsessively checking his nose in a pocket mirror.

It is significant that Ruth Mack Brunswick's case history is as revealing about her own relationship to Freud and to his text, than about her relationship to her patient. First of all, she chose to call her own case history, 'A Supplement to Freud's *History of an Infantile Neurosis*', and instructs the reader to approach her text by first reading Freud's case history. 'All the childhood material appears there; nothing new whatsoever made its appearance in the analysis with me. The source of the new illness was an unresolved remnant of the transference, which, after fourteen years, under the stress of peculiar circumstances, became the basis for a new form of illness'[38] She then proceeds to portray her task as being geared towards resolving the remnants of the Wolf-Man's transference to Freud, and portrays her role as that of 'a mediator between the patient and Freud'.[39] Mack Brunswick, through these self-effacing comments is signalling loud and clear her allegiance to Freud and to his narrative of childhood. However, it is to be noted that her subject matter is in fact different: this second case history tells the story of an unresolved transference. Her narrative uses the dreams that her adult patient brings her, as a support to the line of identification that is being traced between the various doctors sought out in connection with the nose problem, the patient's father and Freud-as-father. Mack Brunswick downplays the significance of the striking female figures who do appear, ambiguous figures with phallic characteristics. She does link them to fantasies of herself, the new analyst, but in the end uses them to bolster the story of the father.[40]

The 'Supplement' is a tale of transference, but an unusually complex one: both patient and analyst are in fact addressing their common analyst, Freud. Mack Brunswick, whilst a disciple and analysand, found herself in the position of having to continue, and by implication, to better, the task begun by her own master and analyst. Mack Brunswick's Hungarian colleague, Jeno Harnik, a member of Ferenczi's circle who had moved to Berlin to teach in the new Institute of Psychoanalysis[41] intervened at precisely this level, taking on the role of a supervisor to his colleague in an article in the *Internationale Zeitschrift für Psychoanalyse*. After praising the paper as one of the most remarkable publications by a follower of Freud,[42] he goes on to challenge her claims to theoretical anonymity. According to Harnik, she is so busy defending Freud, for instance, against the attacks of Rank, who had claimed that the famous wolf-dream referred to the patient's adult world, that she neglects the genuinely new material that she uncovers.[43] He then strikes to the heart of the problem, by stating that her ability to help her patient overcome regressive fantasies is linked precisely to having discovered something new, thereby undermining Freud's authority to the advantage of the patient's actual analyst, Mack Brunswick, herself.[44]

Mack Brunswick replied by reiterating once again that her contribution consisted in a mere replication of Freud's work. The debate extended into the following issue of the journal. Harnik once again insisted on Mack Brunswick's originality. In fact, he even extended the argument by insisting that her paper provides the material ground to connect the wolf-man's neurosis to a disturbance of the oral phase, thereby downplaying the exclusive importance of the Oedipal scenario and the primal scene as aetiological factors for the patient.[45] In her reply, she once again desisted, thereby defending Freud's theoretical groundwork, and placing her allegiance firmly with him.[46]

Freud's case histories in general, and the Wolf-Man case in particular, played a key role in the institutionalisation of psychoanalysis, formulating the terms in which psychoanalysis could be transmitted. The Wolf-Man case needed to, and succeeded in securing the basic tenets of the discipline, the Oedipus Complex and the importance of infantile sexuality, and confirmed them as sound, teachable theories. The debate over Ruth Mack Brunswick's case, between Harnik and Mack Brunswick herself, took place in the context of a psychoanalytic practice well on the road to institutionalisation, and served to highlight the constraints imposed by the terms of transmission. In the years following the creation of the first formal training institutes, psychoanalysts had to negotiate their role within an expanding discipline. They had to fight for their position within a professional community shaped by its very rules of training into a vast family with a genealogy directly traceable to Freud.

I opened this paper with an assumption of the precariousness of psychoanalysis, a precariousness which had something to do with its material: the unconscious and the clinical encounter. It is precisely the nature of this material, I went on to argue, that made for such an awkward partnership between psychoanalysis and history. By sketching the creation of the first analytic institutes, I then tried to show how as institutional formations, they were somehow felt to be at odds with the subject matter that they proposed to teach. Finally, in considering the vicissitudes of the Wolf-man case, and the Freud/Brunswick/Harnik debate, I suggested that case histories as public texts, function *within* institutional formations. It is important to look at them both in terms of their textuality (what kinds of writing they are) and in terms of the psychoanalytic interactions they portray (between patient and analyst and the broader community). In doing so, it is possible to reach the crucial, yet difficult point of interaction between the two: the question of transmission. In certain respects this is a political and institutional (in the broad sense) issue, because it concerns ownership, control over knowledge and the building of communities which will house and regulate that knowledge.

Elizabeth Wright makes this point by framing her essay, 'Transmission in Psychoanalysis and Literature' with two remarkable examples, with which I will end my talk. The first consists in a story, *An Author with a Will of his Own*, by Thomas Bernhard. A playwright's quest to exercise absolute control over his only play leads him to shoot dead the entire first-night audience, which, as audiences do, has not reacted according to the way he had willed. The second example concerns an experiment by a director of the Berliner Ensemble. He had got a random man to stand on a stage doing nothing, yet the audience constructed a compelling story for themselves out of this non-play. As Wright says, the 'struggle for transmission is the struggle to decide whose text it is anyway'.[47] The lesson to be learnt is that the text, ultimately, might well belong to the one who receives it, but any amount of violence can, and is, used in the effort to exercise control over that transmission. Possession, in the end, might well be as illusory as self-possession itself. The lesson for a kind of history telling which proposes to be psychoanalytic is precisely that the archive that it must use is of the most precarious kind, poised between the general and the singular, preservation and destruction.

Notes and Bibliography

1. Eva Brabant, Ernst Falzeder, Patrizia Giaperi-Deutsch (1993) *The Correspondence of Sigmund Freud and Sandor Ferenczi* Vol I, 1908-1914; letter 393, p483. Trans. by Peter Hoffer. Cambridge, Mass. and London: Harvard University Press

2. Joan Copjec ed. (1994) *Supposing the Subject* London: Verso, pVII

3. Roy Porter and Mark Micale eds. (1994) *Discovering the History of Psychiatry* p5. Oxford: O.U.P.

4. Arnold Davidson (1988) 'How to do the History of Psychoanalysis: A Reading of Freud's *Three Essays on the Theory of Sexuality* ' in Francoise Meltzer, ed. *The Trail(s) of Psychoanalysis.* Chicago: University of Chicago Press.

5. Elisabeth Roudinesco (1995) *Genealogies.* Paris: Fayard.

6. Jacques Derrida (1995) *Mal d'Archive*. Paris: Galilée. The book is now available in translation as *Archive Fever* (Chicago University Press 1996, translated by Eric Prenowitz)

7. Roudinesco, p9.

8. Roudinesco, p10.

9. Roudinesco, p101.

10. Yosef Hayim Yerushalmi (1991) *Freud's Moses: Judaism Terminable and Interminable* New Haven: Yale University Press.

11. Derrida, p15.

12. Sigmund Freud and Carl Jung (1974) *The Freud/Jung Letters.* Edited by William McGuire and translated by Ralph Mannheim (Harmondsworth: Penguin, 1991), p59.

13. John Forrester argues that wild analysis is wild because it bypasses precisely this recommendation, Forrester J. *Seductions of Psychoanalysis* (1990), pp241-242.

14. Freud (1912) 'Recommendations to Physicians...' *S.E.XII* p116

15. At a Freud Museum conference in 1994, Juliet Mitchell recounting her transformation from an academic into an analyst, echoed precisely this view of the imponderable authenticity of the analytic experience, which for her involved a move from 'thinking with the mind to thinking with the body'. 'Psychoanalysis and Feminism: 20 years on' *British Journal of Psychotherapy* Vol 12, No. 1

16. By the 1920 congress held at La Hague, offical membership was 62 with 57 guests.

17. Ernest Simmel 'Sur l'histoire et la signification sociale de l'Institut Psychanalytique de Berlin' in Colonomos ed. (1930) *On forme des psychanalystes: Rapport original sur les dix ans de l'Institut Psychanalytique de Berlin 1920-1930,* trans. by Helen Stierlin and Marianne Henich (Paris: Denoel, 1985), pp45-53.

18. Joan Fleming and Therese Benedek (1966) *Psychoanalytic Supervision* (New York & London: Grune and Stratton), p9.

19. Sandor Ferenczi and Otto Rank (1925) *The Development of Psychoanalysis* (1924) (New York & Washington; Nervous and Mental Disease Publishing Co.)

20. Vilma Kovacs (1936) 'Training and Control Analysis' *International Journal of Psychoanalysis* 17 pp346-354, p353.

21. Freud S. (1937) 'Analysis Terminable and Interminable', *S.E.XXIII,* pp216-253, p248.

22. Most recently, it served as the title of a book by Janet Malcolm, which cleverly followed a fictionalised figure of a psychoanalyst through his disillusionment tinged with idealism about his profession. Janet Malcolm (1982) *Psychoanalysis: The Impossible Profession* (London: Karnac, 1988).

23. *S.E. XXIII*, pp217-218.

24. Nicholas Rand (1976) 'Translator's introduction' in Nicolas Abraham and Maria Torok *The Wolf Man's Magic Word; A Cryptonymy* Minneapolis: University of Minnesota Press 1986, ppli-lxxii, plii.

25. S.E. XVII, p7.

26. Peter Gay (1988) *Freud: A Life for Our Times* London: Papermac, 1989, p241.

27. S.E. XVII, p52.

28. Brooks P. (1984) 'Fictions of the Wolf-Man: Freud and narrative understanding' in *Reading for the Plot* Oxford: Blackwell

29. Brooks, p283.

30. Brooks, pp284-285. Patrick Mahony in *Cries of the Wolf-Man* (New York: International U.P. 1984) comes to a similar conclusion about the openness of Freud's 'polyphonic discourse', p160.

31. Stanley Fish (1987) 'Withholding the missing portion: psychoanalysis and rhetoric' in *The Trail(s) of Psychoanalysis*, Francoise Meltzer ed. (Chicago: University of Chicago Press), pp183-209.

32. Fish, p195

33. Fish discusses in a lengthy footnote (p187-188) the considerable literature criticising psychoanalysis for its lack of 'scientificity', from Eysenck's *Uses and Abuses of Psychology*, (Harmondsworth: Penguin, 1953) to Marshall Edelson's *Hypothesis and Evidence in Psychoanalysis* (U. of Chicago Press, 1984). However he takes care not to align himself with these authors, for he ends his essay by positing that it is just as impossible for Freud to stand outside rhetoric as it is impossible for him to stand outside the unconscious. But by virtue of this logic one is moved to ask, where does Fish think he is standing?

34. Fish, p.200.

35. S.E. XVII, pp9-11.

36. See for example the diverging, and often critical readings of the case by psychoanalysts such as Torok and Abraham (1986), Mark Kanzer, 'Wolf-Man: Search for a Primal Scene' and Robert Langs 'The Misalliance dimension on the case of the Wolf-Man' in Kanzer and Glenn (1978) *Freud and his Patients* (New York: Aronson), and Serge Viederman, and the special issue of the *Revue Francaise de*

Psychanalyse dedicated to the Wolf-Man (35, 1971).

37. Paul Roazen (1975) *Freud and His Followers* (London: Allan Lane), pp415-430; Lisa Appignanesi and John Forrester, *Freud's Women* (London: Weidenfeld and Nicholson, 1992), pp373-378.

38. Ruth Mack Brunswick (1928) 'A Supplement to Freud's 'History of an Infantile Neurosis'', *International Journal of Psycho-Analysis* 9 (1928), pp439-477; p440.

39. ibid. p476.

40. See for example on p457 the woman 'wearing trousers and high boots' and 'driving a sleigh in a masterful manner' and p465, 'the page with a blue knickerbocker suit and three-cornered hat'. Mack Brunswick would be one of the first to write about the pre-Oedipal phase, in 'The Analysis of a Case of Paranoia' *J. of Nervous and Mental Diseases* 70 (1929), pp1-22, pp155-79. The ideas were developed in 'The Pre-Oedipal Phase of the Libido Development', *Psychoanalytic Quarterly* 9 (1940), although, in that piece too, she downplays her originality and hands Freud precedence.

41. André Haynal (1988) *The Technique at Issue* (London: Karnac), p46.

42. Jeno Harnik, Ruth Mack Brunswick (1930) 'Diskussionen', *Internationale Zeitschrift für Psychoanalyse* 16, pp123-129.

43. ibid p126. In a famous polemical article Rank had argued that the wolf dream was in fact about the patient's analysis with Freud, with the wolves standing for the disciples in a photograph on Freud's desk.

44. *I.Z.P.*16, 127.

45. Jeno Harnik, Ruth Mack Brunswick (1931) 'Diskussionen', *Internationale Zeitschrift für Psychoanalyse* 17, pp400-402, p402.

46. ibid. p402.

47. Elizabeth Wright (1987) 'Transmission in Psychoanalysis and Literature: Whose Text is it Anyway?' in *Discourse in Psychoanalysis and Literature*, ed. by Shlomith Rimmon-Kenan (London, Methuen), pp90-193, p102.

Using the Case Study in the Assessment of Trainees

Laurence Spurling

(1) THE CASE STUDY IN PSYCHOTHERAPY

In this paper I want to look at the presentation of case material in the context of teaching, and particularly assessment in the training of psychodynamic practitioners. I will draw mainly on my experience of teaching on a psychodynamic counselling course, on which my students are required to write an account of their work with clients in the form of a case study as part of their assessment. Let me say that, for the purposes of this paper, I will use the terms 'counselling', 'psychotherapy' and 'psychoanalysis' interchangeably, and by 'counselling' or 'psychotherapy' I will always mean in the psychodynamic tradition.

In considering this I want first of all to highlight several features of the presentation of case material in clinical discourse.

(i) Privacy

The first thing I want to say is obvious but important: the practice of psychotherapy is carried out in privacy. Freud discusses this in his *Introductory Lectures*. What takes place in a psychoanalytic treatment, he says, is an 'interchange of words', and to learn about psychoanalysis it would be good if we could listen to what passes between an analyst and patient.

> *But we cannot do that [either]. The talk of which psychoanalytic treatment consists brooks no listener; it cannot be demonstrated. A neurasthenic or hysterical patient can of course, like any other, be introduced to students in a psychiatric lecture. He will give an account of his complaints and symptoms, but of nothing else. The information required by analysis will be given by him only on condition of his having special emotional attachment to the doctor; he would become silent as soon as he observed a single witness to whom he felt indifferent. For this information concerns what is most intimate in his mental life, everything that, as a homogeneous personality, he will not admit to himself.*
>
> *Thus you cannot be present as an audience at a psychoanalytic treatment. You can only be told about it; and, in the strictest sense of the word, it is only by hearsay that you will get to know psychoanalysis* (S.E. XV 17-18)

Thus instruction in psychoanalysis can only be 'second hand'. This is a fundamental feature of our profession: we never really know what each of us gets up to with our patients.

This is one reason why clinical presentations are often such charged, emotional occasions. They offer the hope of communicating to our colleagues what we cannot show them, of putting a professionally sanctioned breach in our rule of confidentiality, of overcoming the isolation and loneliness to which we are condemned by the need for privacy in our profession.

(ii) Integration of Theory and Practice

The case presentation, either as a verbal presentation or as a written communication, seems to be the ideal medium for the communication of psychoanalysis as it takes place, as it were, at the crossroads of theory and practice. There is, I think, a constant strain in bringing together theoretical ideas, concepts and systems with clinical realities. The case presentation offers a format in which theory can be integrated with practice and turned into coherent communication.

(iii) Openness and Incompleteness of Clinical Discourse

Out of this need for convivial colleagueship, the presentation of clinical material to colleagues can be an occasion for lively and creative discussion. A space is created in which, out of the interchange between presenter and audience, new meanings, and new aspects of transference and counter-transference may come to light. This is explored in David Tuckett's paper 'Some Thoughts on the Presentation and Discussion of the Clinical Material of Psychoanalysis' (*Int. J. Psycho-Analysis* 1993 Vol 74, pp1175-1189), in which he argues that the clinical presentation is an essentially open and partial communication, requiring the audience's response to the paper, and the manner of its actual delivery, to complete the process. It is in the nature of a sensitive and thoughtful account of a piece of work that the unformed or half-formed thoughts, ideas and constructions will be present or implicit in the text of which the author is not aware. As Tuckett observes:

> *We have [then] a rather curious situation. The analyst, however skilled and distinguished he may be and with many hours of dedication and thought behind him in his work with the patient, finds that colleagues with none of this investment or experience, or perhaps even his skill, are very likely to detect new and important meanings in the material that he has not seen.* (p1185)

(iv) Case Study as Ideological

However, historically the case presentation particularly in its written form, has been given another function. In the introduction to the Dora case, for example, Freud wrote that the case would 'substantiate' his views on hysteria and the formation of hysterical symptoms (SE VII p7). In a similar way Klein states her belief that the case of Richard in *Narrative of a Child Analysis* (Virago Press, 1989) enabled her to 'confirm a number of my theoretical conclusions' (p14). The case presentation is now no longer an invitation to a dialogue with the reader, but charged with confirming, giving clinical proof of theoretical ideas. The reader is not, if you like, on equal footing, but now becomes a silent witness to this demonstration on Freud's or Klein's part.

The use of the case presentation to substantiate and confirm theoretical ideas has been subjected to a sustained critique. The point is that the case study, by its very nature as a piece of narrative, cannot carry this weight as a kind of laboratory test of theoretical or clinical ideas. Modern writers are therefore chary of invoking this function of the case presentation.

(2) TEACHING PSYCHODYNAMIC THERAPY: TEACHER AS GATEKEEPER

I will now turn to consider some aspects of the teaching of psychoanalytic practice. If, in Freud's phrase, both psychoanalysis and education are 'impossible professions', it is not surprising that teaching the psychoanalytic approach is subject to considerable strain. The particular tension I want to focus on can be illustrated by a not infrequent occurrence when I am presenting a theoretical system or outlook for the first time. A student will ask me 'do I have to believe this?' Now the question may be asked out of anxiety, puzzlement, arrogance or fear. My concern here is not to consider why the question is asked, but to consider what a truthful answer might be.

It is not that a ready, and quite satisfactory answer can't be found. I can speak, and do speak of the value in learning of suspending belief and disbelief, of taking theoretical systems not necessarily as concrete reality but metaphorical constructions, and so on. But, as has often been pointed out, it is also true to say that the history of psychoanalysis is in many ways one of power struggles over what one might call the true beliefs of psychoanalysis. Freud was always quite clear that to be counted as a psychoanalyst meant 'accepting' certain 'cornerstones' of psychoanalytic theory - he had in mind the existence of unconscious mental processes, the theory of sexuality and the Oedipus complex. Although we may today disagree with what those cornerstones are, I think those who teach on a recognised course - whether it is an official professional training, or, like the counselling course I am speaking of, a more indirect route to professional qualification - are gatekeepers to the profession, charged with admitting only those who demonstrate both competence and commitment to the psychodynamic tradition.

The privacy of our work engenders, I think, a pervasive anxiety about whether it conforms to the psychoanalytic canon. Any clinical presentation made by one practitioner to another always, in some form or another, carries the need to re-affirm one's membership, and right to be a member, of the psychoanalytic community. Each time a clinical presentation is made, and the participants survive, the ghost of the wild analyst can once again, at least for the time being, be laid to rest.

To return to the student's question: 'do I have to believe this?' I think a truthful answer is rather equivocal. Psychoanalytic practice is not really about belief. When, for instance, Bion speaks of the psychoanalyst's 'faith', he does not mean something that can be deduced from adherence to certain beliefs, but the courage to commit oneself to something which cannot be spelt out in advance. 'Commitment' is a more active process than 'believing'. But psychoanalysis can and does get reduced to a series of beliefs, notably when politics and power come into play.

(3) THE CASE STUDY IN TEACHING PSYCHODYNAMIC THERAPY

With this equivocation in mind, I will turn to the use of case presentations in teaching and assessment. On the course I teach on, (and I am sure this is true of most courses), the case presentation is made in two different ways: verbally in a case discussion group, and in a written form as part of the formal assessment process.

a. Case discussion groups, a group of about five students and one tutor, are conducted in the open critical spirit of clinical discourse. Class discussion, if all goes well, is truly a discussion, a dialogue between the presenter and the tutor and the other group members in which sense is made together of what might be at issue in the particular case presented.

Here the demands of teaching, in its most formal sense of imparting knowledge in one form or another, are at their minimum. Here my role as gatekeeper is not lost, but more loosely held. If teaching necessarily involves the transmission of a tradition, the case discussion group offers the best opportunity for this tradition to be experienced and re-discovered: not only for the students but for the teachers as well.

Take, for instance, the question of boundaries that constantly come up in case presentations: should the student answer the client's question about his or her private life, should a gift be accepted, and so on? The most satisfying way to conduct the group - and the one most true to the psychoanalytic spirit of free enquiry - is for me as tutor to 'forget', put in brackets all my knowledge and experience of the importance of maintaining boundaries, and, if I am feeling particularly bold, of even putting into question the point of thinking of practice in this territorial language. I am then free to convince myself anew that, yes, there is a point in thinking of practice in terms of boundaries, and yes, it is a good idea to have boundaries worth keeping. Only when I have successfully convinced myself will I effectively convince the students.

b. As well as giving verbal case presentations in class, students are also required to present cases in a written form for assessment. This formal piece of work, known as the case study, is handed to the tutors who then write comments, assign a mark, and hand back the case study, with the comments and mark, to the student.

Clearly the openness and incompleteness of the clinical discourse no longer holds. It is like the lively process of a clinical meeting has become frozen into a series of disjointed steps which do not allow for dialogue and discussion. In the written case study students have to describe their work and their thinking about their work, but they also have to prove to their readers that they are capable of working at a satisfactory level. The tutor, who is able to relax his or her position of authority in the clinical discourse, now becomes 'the one who knows', who has to have some pre-existing standard of competence and commitment against which the written case study is judged.

Here we see a version enacted of what I have called the *ideological function* of the case presentation, one generally discredited in the profession. The student is put in a position where he or she has to persuade, to substantiate a point of view, to prove a good enough theoretical knowledge and understanding. The tutor is put in a position of demanding this of the student, and determining its success or otherwise.

(4) THE PLACE OF KNOWLEDGE

Now these are not the only criteria in play when the written case study becomes part of a formal assessment. There *is* a way in which the student's knowledge and understanding of psychoanalytic theory, technique and practices is put to the test. For instance, there are fairly clear ways a student can write about or use aspects of psychodynamic theory - say the difference between the paranoid-schizoid and depressive position - and show whether they have understood or failed to understand the theoretical ideas employed.

What I an saying is that this sense of assessing something factual or demonstrable - which is sometimes expressed in terms of the correct and incorrect 'application' of theory showing whether that theory has been understood or not - is not the only thing that happens in the assessment of cases studies, and in my view is not the primary thing.

I will give an illustration of what I have in mind. I will take it from another part of the formal assessment where factual knowledge would seem to be at a premium, the written, unseen *exam* which, as a university masters course, we are obliged to set. One of the questions we have set, and may continue to set, is: 'what is the Oedipus complex?'. In answering the question, the student will be asked to illustrate his or her answer with clinical examples.

Now what would be a satisfactory answer to this question? Of course the student would have to have read some Freud, and probably some other theorists in order to put together an answer, and it is not difficult to compile in advance certain ideas or formulations which should appear in order for the student to pass.

But this is to reduce the question to a very concrete level. In their *Dictionary of Psychoanalysis* (Hogarth Press, 1973) Laplanche and Pontalis make two pertinent comments about the Oedipus complex. They observe that the history of Freud's elaboration and development of the concept of the Oedipus complex 'is really coextensive with that of psychoanalysis itself'. They also point out that Freud nowhere gave a systematic account of it.

Fools rush in where angels fear to tread. In requiring our students to become fools, to spell out what the Oedipus complex is, we are putting them in a position where they have to make up for Freud's studied reticence, go beyond it, correct it. In so doing, they are having to give an account of psychoanalysis itself, or, more accurately, *their* version of psychoanalysis itself.

(5) LANGUAGE AS PERFORMATIVE: THE CASE STUDY AS DEMONSTRATION OF COMMITMENT.

When it comes to the written case study, this is much clearer. The student is not only or simply describing a piece of work 'out there', the quality of which the tutors try to assess. The account of the work is a narrative of which the student is the author. What is being assessed is the nature and quality of the version of psychoanalysis constructed.

Language thus functions not only as descriptive, but as *performative*, as a series of what philosophers of language have called *speech acts*. In a speech act, uttering a sentence is itself the performance of what the sentence is about, as in promising to do something. And so, as author of their version of psychoanalysis, students are at the same time demonstrating their commitment to psychoanalysis, and the nature and quality of this commitment is being assessed.

Again I can try to illustrate this by taking some examples. Suppose a student, in the course of giving some factual information about his or her client in terms of age, sex, marital status and so on, writes of a female client that 'six months ago she reluctantly separated from her husband because of his long-standing drinking problem'.

Now this way of describing a client would raise in my mind the question: how does the student *know* that the client separated 'reluctantly'? Did the client tell the counsellor, and if so what did the counsellor make of this communication? Or did the counsellor assume or infer this reluctance on the client's part, and on what evidence?

The simple point I wish to make is that in the writer's description something is glossed over which should be given attention, namely the counsellor's position vis-à-vis the client (and, at the same time, the writer's position vis-à-vis the reader). The distinction between client and counsellor, between what the client might say and what the counsellor might think, has been elided.

This might seem a very minor point, but it does address what

I think is crucial here: that what is being assessed in a case study is whether the student has created a medium or space in which thought, reflection and self-appraisal can take place. This attitude on the part of the practitioner is a vital part of what we call psychodynamic practice. This has been expressed in countless ways by the key figures in the dynamic tradition. So for instance Winnicott, in *The Maturational Processes and the Facilitating Environment* (1965, Hogarth Press. Reprinted 1990, Karnac books) put it like this:

> .... *in between the patient and the analyst is the analyst's professional attitude, his technique,* the work he does with his mind. (p161)

This is what we aim to assess: the student's professional attitude, the work done with his mind.

Let me give another example. Suppose a student writes something like this, in the course of a description of a particular session with a client:

> *Mrs A [the client] began to cry, with increasing intensity. I was beginning to feel uneasy with her loss of control, and wondered if I was going to be able to contain her. Mrs A continued to speak of how depressed she was, how she felt she had nothing in her life. I attempted to acknowledge her distress; she was unable to hear my attempts to empathize with her. I started to speculate whether I was finding myself acting as Mrs A's own mother had done when faced with her daughter's depression.*

The issue I want to address is this: is this extract a demonstration of a struggle to understand and work with this client, an honest record of the counsellor's feelings and reactions to the client and an attempt to work out an aspect of the transference? Or is there here a recourse to psychoanalytic and counselling cliché, in which language functions as a substitute for and defence against thought and sensibility?

In order to answer these questions we have to rely on our own critical sensibility in appraising the text. So in this example, we might first want to consider the following. Firstly, the words 'containing' and 'empathizing' seem to be used as transitive verbs, as something one does. Is this an unsophisticated use of these terms, or might it reflect a tendency towards over-simplification, an inappropriate concreteness or literalness on the writer's part, as though one can learn *how* to contain, empathize, become a transference-figure and so on, and then simply apply this learning in the counselling situation? Secondly the student seems to write as though what he or she is doing in the counselling could be transparent, could be appraised at the time, rather than something which necessarily only happens in retrospect.

What I think would happen is that a tutor reading a text in which the above extract is typical would register something about the professional attitude of the writer. It probably would be formulated in a different language - for example, transference and counter-transference. But it comes down to the student's particular use of language.

In unguarded moments I sometimes feel that I can judge a case study after reading no more than the first paragraph. This arrogance on my part is a recognition that, from the opening words of the essay, the student is situating himself or herself as the author of the account which will follow, and that this is being registered by me. There is an obvious analogy with the way patients first present themselves to the therapist or counsellor being a good guide of how they will conduct themselves in the therapy.

(6) RHETORIC AND THE CASE STUDY

What follows from what I am arguing is that there is a much closer link between clinical and literary sensibility than is generally recognized in the teaching and assessment of counselling and therapy. What does not seem to be discussed, for instance, is what view of language we hold to in assessing the written case study. I think in practice we take a view of language which is distinctly unmodern, or pre-modern. We tend to consider language to be transparent, the vehicle through which the student's thinking and feeling will shine through, which itself is taken as a sign, albeit at several removes, of his or her actual counselling work.

There is a belief, or maybe a hope, that in his or her writing the student will reveal him or herself as fit or unfit to enter the psychoanalytic community. Good practice will show itself in good writing, and bad practice in bad writing. This view of language is similar to that of the ancient rhetoricians regarding speech, in which felicity in speech was taken as an outward sign of inward understanding and virtue. In the words of Isocrates, adviser to

Alexander the Great:

> *The power to speak well is taken as the surest index of a sound understanding, and discourse which is true and lawful and just is the outward image of a good and faithful soul.*

This gives rise to an image which haunts the course I work on (and probably other trainings): that of the student who can pervert or subvert language, where language does not reveal but deceives, whose academic or technical skill in using psychoanalytic language covers up a lack or deficit in the basic emotional capacities needed to become a counsellor. This figure, made up of bits of actual students mixed in with phantasies, projections and fears of the staff, represents what the course fears most, its 'shadow'. This shadow-figure has a rather paradoxical relationship to the case study. As a university course, the written case study takes its place with several other forms of assessment, such as written exams and theoretical essays. The hope is that the case study, as that form of assessment most suited to counselling as representing the *integration* of theoretical knowledge with clinical practice, will 'catch' these figures out; there is a belief that their unsuitability as counsellors will reveal itself in ways they cannot control, just as the patient's unconscious will reveal itself in the consulting room.

But such a figure also represents the other side of rhetoric, and one which is much more modern. So John Locke, in *An Essay Concerning Human Understanding* writes:

> *We must allow that all the Art of Rhetorick, besides Order and Clearness, all the artificial and figurative application of Words Eloquence hath invented, are for nothing else but to insinuate wrong ideas, move the Passions, and thereby misleade the Judgement; and so indeed are perfect cheat.*

In more clinical language, David Tuckett makes a similar point:

> *There is the possibility that a good, well-told and coherent story creates the risk of seduction, which in the context of communication to others can be summed up thus: the more a narrative is intellectually, emotionally and aesthetically satisfying, the better it incorporates clinical events into rich and sophisticated patterns, the less space is left to the audience to notice alternative patterns and to elaborated alternative narratives.* (Tuckett 1993, p1183)

(7) THE DISPLACEMENT OF CLINICAL DISCOURSE

By way of conclusion I want to return to consider again what I have called the strain involved in using the presentation of case material for purposes of assessment. I have argued that, in the formal process of assessing a written case study, a return to the more conservative and ideological aspects of our tradition is enacted, in which the student has to use his or her written account to prove his knowledge and competence, and the tutor has to become both witness and judge of this.

The uneasiness of this position for the tutor can be seen in a conflict I find myself in when I mark a written case study handed in to me. In my written comments about the work, which will be given back to the student together with the essay, I have noticed that I am never quite sure how to address the student whose work I am marking, and who is known to me as someone I teach on the course.

Is the student to be addressed directly, as in the form: 'in this case study *you* have succeeded in showing / failed to show...'. Or is it more appropriate for an indirect, third-person form of address to be used, to speak of 'the author', or 'this essay' demonstrates / fails to demonstrate a clear understanding of...'? Neither seems right: to address the student as 'you' seems to turn the assessment process into a collaborative supervisory relationship, to invite dialogue where the opportunity does not allow one. On the other hand not to address the student directly, which is the appropriate model for a formal assessment in which personal knowledge of the student is seen as a barrier to impartiality, seems to institute a pretence that the writer is unknown to me.

How, then, can the freshness and creativity of a clinical discussion which takes place in the presentation of case material find a place in this formal assessment process? How can the strain of teaching and assessment find some relief? I think this dialogue - between presenter and audience in the clinical context, between teacher and student in the teaching context - becomes one between tutor and tutor in the assessment context.

On our course the teaching unit is always a group of four tutors, who meet to determine what mark will be given to each student. In these meetings the markers of each piece of work (there are always two markers) each 'presents' their judgment to their colleagues. Out of this discussion a decision is arrived at about the mark assigned to each piece of work.

These assessment meetings (which can happen in more or less formal contexts) clearly function as a brake on individual prejudice and as a serious and responsible attempt to be as impartial as possible. My point here is that they also function as a way of keeping alive, of preserving the medium of discourse, of dialogue, which is an essential feature of the case presentation.

If we try to know more about how case presentation in clinical discourse can embody originality and freshness rather than orthodoxy and deadness, when it comes to the teaching and assessment of psychodynamic practice the focus needs to shift to the teaching unit itself as a subject of study, the sum of relationships between the tutors and the institution in which they work.

Case Reports and the Reality they Represent: The Many Faces of *Nachträglichkeit*

Donald P. Spence

> *And so each venture*
> *Is a new beginning, a raid on the inarticulate*
> *With the shabby equipment always deteriorating*
> *In the general mess of imprecision of feeling,*
> *Undisciplined squads of emotion.*
> T.S. Eliot, *Burnt Norton*

One of the central arguments in Grünbaum's early critique of psychoanalysis (Grünbaum, 1984) focused on the importance of the analyst's suggestions in directing the flow of free associations. If free associations were partly directed by the analyst's evolving theory of the case, then they were not really free and even more troubling, the clinical material that forms the basis of our psychoanalytic literature speaks with more than the patient's voice. It was entirely possible, argued Grünbaum, for each piece of clinical data to be 'more or less alike confounded by the analyst's suggestion so as to conform to his construction, at the cost of their epistemic reliability or probative value. For example, a 'confirming' early memory may be compliantly produced by the patient on the heels of giving docile assent to an interpretation' (Grünbaum 1984, p277)

Raising the possibility of undue influence in this and other ways has had the useful consequence of forcing analysts to turn to the verbatim transcripts of the case and uncover specific instances of suggestion (see Spence 1987). It has fuelled a new interest in process research and sensitized researchers to the way in which the analyst can impose a story line on the patient's productions and in this way, turn them into supporting evidence for received theory. Far from being free, these associations are sometimes (and perhaps frequently) being directed by the analyst's own agenda; as a result of this damaging possibility, case reports are being more carefully scrutinized and several proposals have been advanced to improve their evidential standing (see Klumpner and Frank, 1991).

Less attention has been paid to another kind of narrative smoothing which takes place as the clinical material is being prepared for publication. The analyst may be perfectly correct in his responses to the patient and never make the mistake of suggesting alternative story lines or, in other respects, 'leading the witness', but we have no control over the way the clinical material is changed - rethought or re-remembered - on the way to publication. Thus a brief allusion to an Oedipal theme during the session may be sharpened to a much stronger support for a popular position than is warranted by the clinical events of the treatment.

Probably the best documented example of this kind of memory mistake comes from Kubie (1958). A supervisee came in one day for a session and apologised for the fact that his notes were incomplete because, in the middle of the session, the patient had asked him to turn off the tape recorder. The supervisor suggested they play the tape anyway; it was played up to the interruption when the voice of the therapist could be clearly heard asking that the machine be turned of. The therapist had no memory of this incident.

There is an irony in drawing attention to the way our memory is less than perfect because it rests on a phenomenon that we often see in our clinical work. We are fascinated as clinicians by the way in which context can affect memory and we know from long experience how minor (and sometimes major) changes in how something is remembered can be brought about by changes in a patient's mood or by changes in the transference. Because we see this contamination happening all the time in our clinical work, I think we may be less concerned about the way it may operate in our more scientific activities. But the implications are clearly quite different. While we may learn from each new version of a favourite memory something about the tone of the transference or (if we are lucky) some new facet of the original happening, quite a different consequence emerges when we substitute a wished-for clinical happening for the original event. This kind of narrative smoothing can obviously (and silently) erode the foundations of psychoanalytic theory or what the analyst/author may prefer for what the evidence happens to be. When case reports are too frivolously shaded by these constraints, theory will never change because it is always being 'supported' by the facts; under these conditions, we will never discover anything new because the unexpected fact is always being forgotten or turned into what theory demands. The Zeitgeist, and in particular, fashionable theory, determines the 'evidence' - not, as is standard, the other way around.

In extreme cases, it could be argued that the pleasure principle is in danger of displacing the reality principle; the distinction between what happened and what might have happened becomes blurred. But the danger is even greater because the therapist is usually the only witness; if we don't trust his or her version of the clinical happening, we have nowhere else to turn.

In the worst possible case, the case report is pure primary process - a published dream. Consider the parallels between the average dream and the average case report. Both are unverifiable accounts of one-time happenings with either no witnesses (in the dream), or one witness (the patient) who is normally not permitted to speak or publish. Both dreams and case reports are triggered by recent, actual events (day residues or clinical happenings) which are largely unverifiable and must be taken on faith. They are both subject to the laws of the primary process; at worst, they are both examples of wish-fulfilling narratives. But whereas the dream is typically used as an excuse for further associations and is almost never taken as a true account of how things are, the case report is typically accepted as a reliable description of recent clinical happenings and for that reason given space in almost every copy of the three principle psychoanalytic journals. Yet even though the case report has far more evidential standing than the dream, the formal properties of these two genres are more similar than different.

In drawing your attention to these dangers, I am trying to make you aware of how little we really know about the truth value of the average case report and how easily it can be adjusted (often unwittingly) to meet the needs of the author. We are fully aware of the wish-fulfilling potential of the average dream; why are we so gullible in the face of the average case report? Knowing what we do about the way in which actual memories can be rearranged to suit the needs of the rememberer, why are we so willing to accept the case report as a story of what actually happened?

To examine the influence of context on content, I want to take a careful look at three accounts of an early memory:

The patient was a 42 year old man who entered analysis after finding that his wife had had an affair; the target memory was a representation of his circumcision at the age of seven and the events leading up to this moment. He told three different versions of this event. In the first account, he remembers being 'tenderly taken by his mother to the doctor's office. The all-knowing, kind doctor examined the patient' and carried out the circumcision. The second memory took place during a time in the analysis when he experienced the analyst as a bad vindictive father. In this context, he remembered being taken to the doctor 'for hygienic reasons... (his mother) wanted the redness and irritation around his glans penis to be taken care of. The doctor was harsh in his demeanor. He seemed to be viciously delighting in hurting the patient'. The third memory emerged after a session when the analyst was a few minutes early in announcing the end of the hour. The patient returned the next day to say that the analyst had cut him off. Later in the hour, he retold of his circumcision. In this memory, the patient 'somehow knew that his mother knew that he was masturbating. In order to 'show him' the consequences of such a vile practice, she grabbed him by the arm and dragged him through the town to the doctor's office. She 'ordered' the doctor to perform a circumcision which the doctor did. The patient in telling the story, grabbed his genitals and writhed in pain, as he relived the painful, healing period. He had for three years in the analysis 'not seen' the paper towels folded and stacked at the head of the couch. He had recently asked whether they had been there all along. He imagined that they might be diapers or bandages, bloody bandages that he now remembered painfully' (all quotes from Coleman, unpub: pp13-14).

Now it would be an obvious tactical mistake to cross-question the patient to try to find out, each time a new memory emerged, what part of the account was the 'true' version and what part was a fabrication. To proceed in this way would quickly make the patient think twice about saying anything that was slightly problematic; associations would no longer be free; and the analysis would be turned into an exercise in accurate remembering. We let the memory take the form it likes best and trust that we can learn from each new appearance something about the contextual forces at play in the analysis. But wearing our other hat, as we write and publish accounts of our cases that will forever represent, for the reader, the putatively true description of what happened during a particular case, we need to sharpen our sense of the difference between 'might have' and 'must have been' and develop some inner standard - some perfect pitch for the past - that will help us to leave in the clinical happenings we can reasonably verify and leave out the secondary associations.

In one of his early letters to Fliess (No. 52, written in Dec. 6 1896), Freud sketched out the germ of the process we now call *nachträglichkeit*:

> *As you know, I am working on the assumption that our psychical mechanism has come into being by a process of stratification: the material present in the form of memory traces being subjected from time to time to a rearrangement in accordance with fresh circumstances — to a retranscription.* (Masson 1985, p208).

We have just seen three examples of this process in the different versions of the circumcision memory, three examples of *nachträglichkeit*. The mood of the moment seems to influence the patient's recall of an earlier happening, changing important details and their surrounding emotional tone in a way that makes the memory more syntonic with contingent events. What I want to ask is this: Can we also apply the concept of *nachträglichkeit* to published accounts of clinical happenings? If we substitute author for patient and case report for recurring memory, we might ask, to what extent can our (often unconscious) rhetorical, personal and political goals influence our account of the clinical material?

The extreme case is quite easy to define. Suppose a therapist is convinced of a hard and fast link between early child abuse and later pathology; we can easily understand how this conviction might influence his or her memory and presentation of the clinical matters. It could be argued that some of the hysteria around child abuse stems from the exaggerated, often sensational and largely unverified descriptions of patients that fill the case reports of the true believers.

A close reading of the more extreme cases can identify instances where the author's argument seems to jump ahead of the evidence; one such case appears in a paper by Williams, 1987, titled 'Reconstruction of an early seduction and its after effects'. The clinical material pointing to an early seduction is more suggestive than conclusive, resting as it does on repetitive dreams of ugly buildings, overflowing toilets, floating faeces, etc. But no dream is ever reported verbatim. And although the patient remembers going to the home of a favourite family servant and recalls how relatives told him how attached he was to the servant and how he followed him around such memories are merely consistent with a possible seduction; they add nothing to its proof. Throughout her presentation, the author fails to show any evidence of a sceptical mind at work.

Not only is the seduction hypothesis never examined in a critical manner, but its status changes, over the course of the paper, from hypothesis to fact. On page 152, the author describes her suspicion that the patient had been seduced. But on the next page we are told of 'the seduction of Joseph' with no qualification; further references to the 'seduction' occur repeatedly through the article, in the title, and in the abstract. In the next-to-last paragraph, we are told that the 'seduction' (now a simple fact) 'hindered his freedom to develop normally; he lived in shackles until he learned to remove them' (p163).

The possibility of early seduction by the male servant at a time when the father had left home, the mother was away on an extended trip, and the patient was left in the care of elderly relatives seems a plausible hypothesis which could explain the repetitive dreams, the patient's fear of closeness, and other aspects of his symptom picture. It thus ranks as a possible but not a necessary cause of the clinical details, but the distinction between the two is never examined in depth. We have the impression that a little too much narrative smoothing is taking place and that the story line of the case is beginning to conform a little too well to the standard seduction subplot.

For another example of how hypothesis slides too quickly into fact, consider a recent paper by Almond titled 'The analytic role' (Almond 1995). As desirable features of this role, he lists such traits as neutrality, abstinence, curiosity, forthrightness, minimal either/or thinking, analysing-not-reacting, and helpfulness. But nowhere in the paper is there any evidence that these traits actually produce a more useful clinical result or - the converse - that the absence of the traits necessarily does the patient significant harm. All that Almond provides by way of evidence are such statements as 'psychoanalytic theories of mind provide the analyst with a special framework for listening' (p473) or 'psychoanalytic training provides two sorts of information about how to act in the clinical situation' (p475). At no point in the paper does he make an effort to examine treatments in which one or more of the recommended ingredients is conspicuously missing. By failing to develop an evidential case for the kind of role he is recommending, Almond moves quickly from *ought* to *is*. A close reading of the paper shows that the benefits of the described role are simply listed; they are not derived inductively from a close look at different clinical styles. We may overlook this defect in the paper because we feel flattered to read that such desirable traits are attributed to us and do not stop and wonder about the evidence.

This kind of propagandist reporting follows a fairly predictable story line and as we learn the plot, it becomes all the easier to spot. But these examples represent only the tip of the iceberg. Subtler versions of this same kind of distortion, using the same kinds of primary-process mechanisms, may be at work on a lesser scale, going on all the time, slowly and insidiously tilting our understanding of the analytic encounter away from what actually happened, away from the unexpected and truly surprising, toward the politically and clinically correct - and toward what is, more often than not, totally predictable.

You can see that the influence of some personal agenda on the clinical account is closely related to the influence of theory. It is becoming a commonplace these days to point out how theory constrains our view of the clinical happening. The interpersonal or relational analyst who focuses on intrapsychic happenings will almost certainly report a different kind of session than the analyst who focuses on the patient's unconscious. Analysts with the first process model will actually see and hear the material differently from analysts with the second. We are vaguely aware of these constraints and try to take them into account by reading case reports from an interpersonal psychoanalytic journal somewhat differently than from a more classical journal, but in reality, we have few reliable methods for separating fact from fiction. Because the target happening is almost never captured verbatim, we usually have no idea of what kinds of distortions take place and how one analyst's sense of a session differs from another's. About all we know for certain is that a certain kind of bias is probably operating, but we have no way of knowing which facts to discount.

Nor do we have any clear picture of what the patient hears the analyst say and this is a blind spot in most of our verbatim records. We may have the actual words spoken by the analyst but we have usually no idea of how they sound, their timing, inflection , intonation, and all the other subtle features that turn words into speech.

So we are being misled on at least three levels when we read a case report. We are forced to take another author's version as the true account; second, we are fooled into believing that our voicing of the words corresponds to the true voicing, even though the original key and metre may be quite different from our particular favourites; and third, we are tempted to believe that our hearing of the material (and particularly of the analyst's remarks) corresponds to what the patient hears. We project onto the patient our own sense of what is happening and fail to take account of the very real differences between us and them.

There is a fourth mistake we make all the time. Case reports, because they are published documents, are designed to focus on the content of the interchange and not the form - the words and not the music. Yet any number of patients have remarked on the fact that at certain times during their treatment, it was the sound of the analyst's voice that made all the difference and not what he was saying. We begin to realise that the importance of content is always oscillating during the clinical hour and that a properly marked transcript might tell us when the words were largely peripheral and when they start to come back into focus. Suppose we had a way of indicating this transition on the record; think how exciting such a transcript would seem! We would be in a position to recapture the experience of the patient as he or she was listening for the first time. And think how humbling this would be; such a transcript would make us realize that much of what we say is probably never heard in the first place.

And finally, the usual case report says nothing about what is taking place inside the analyst's head. What he or she is thinking in the midst of a particular clinical happening can easily colour how this event is heard and understood. The analyst who is about to leave for vacation tends to hear all references to separation as references to the vacation, and they might easily evoke various degrees of guilt or relief. The analyst who is about to raise his fee tends to hear all references to money as pointing to the change in fee; once again, perception is coloured by context. But the reader usually knows nothing about these transient, contextual events and what is more, tends to substitute his or her own context for what has actually taken place, thus further complicating the picture.

So the plot thickens. To make matters worse, as I have noted in several places, we are entirely at the mercy of the analyst/author who is reporting the case. Other disciplines are in much more fortunate positions. The historian always has the diary or the bill of lading or the act of congress to refer back to; the art historian usually can locate the painting or, at worst, the slide. And even though there are fierce debates among art historians as to how much detail is lost in going from original painting to a slide, at least the slide captures the critical details of the painting and something of the overall Gestalt (although it is edifying in this connection to read what kind of information is lost in the substitution). But we do not even have slides; we have what Lincoln called the mystic chords of memory which cannot be seen or heard, only talked about and then fleetingly.

Having said all this, I will probably surprise you when I conclude that the answer does not lie in more tape recordings or time lapsed video images. We are gradually coming to see that these aids to memory (bringing accuracy of a certain kind) only take us out of the clinical moment and make us less able to understand the 'Why' of a particular intervention. Tuckett, in a recent issue of the

International Journal of Psychoanalysis (Tuckett, 1993), describes a patient who periodically would stop listening to her analyst. At first she would admit to having only a vague sense of his meaning but then admitted that she was having various thoughts of her own during the time he was speaking (1994, p1165). This kind of tuning out would be seriously misrepresented by the average transcript which might present Tuckett's words and then the analysand's response, with all parts of the dialogue having the appearance of a normal conversation. The most important piece of this conversation, of course, is never shown - the patient's unverbalised thoughts.

The fact that the patient was able to break off contact in this way became one of the central themes of the analysis. The patient seemed to feel that 'emotional engagements with (the analyst), a real meeting between patient and analyst is trapping and therefore, pointless; it just creates bad feelings' (p1167). Viewing the analyst as dangerous and at times irrational, the best response is not to listen - to tune him out and have her own thoughts.

Tuckett tries to bring us into the picture by presenting a series of moments when he felt unable to engage or make contact with the patient. Between sessions, he began to clarify his sense of what was happening, and each new understanding was further clarified by the next engagement. We are carried along with him in his episodic discovery of this patient's fear of true contact; as his awareness increases, his formulation becomes more precise; as his language sharpens, so does our understanding. The emerging genre is something like a Henry James short story in which relatively little happens on the surface, but the reader is allowed access to the author's speculations on the other characters' strange behaviour - their silences, their non-sequitors, their unexplained appetites, etc.

Just as this emerging genre may be the best container for the complicated mixture of speech and silence that takes place during an hour, so it is also one of the better ways of engaging our respect and our sense that 'Yes, this is how it must have happened'. Part of the sense of verisimilitude comes from the fact that the narrative is not seamless and that the author / analyst is making all the obvious mistakes (including common errors of interpretation). Part of the emerging trust we feel stems from the sense that the analyst is gradually getting closer to the patient's way of seeing the world;

thus the formulation seems to emerge from the clinical material and not be something imposed from the outside. This part of our understanding is reinforced if the formulation seems somewhat novel and appears to be emerging for the first time.

Another trend worth noting in current case reports is what might be called the greater importance of the relationship. Facts are no longer lying around in the patient's associations, waiting to be interpreted; rather, facts are jointly constructed by patient and analyst. Sometimes the joint enterprise seems to go nowhere; sometimes we are appalled by what seems like the analyst's wrong ideas; and sometimes a work of art is created which puts into words something the patient has known but could never express (Bollas' 'unthought known'). In each of these joint encounters, we get the sense that quite a different discovery would have taken place had a different analyst been in the room and it is simply not true (or at least happens rarely) that we interpret something that is almost in consciousness but not yet expressed. Much more frequently, what we construct is something we assemble in the moment; the old archaeological metaphor of digging up ever-deeper layers of the mind seems finally to have seen its day. The new case material makes us aware of how active the analyst must be in creating his sense of the patient's truth at that time and place and how much depends on finding the right language to express it.

This new sense of the analyst as linguistic architect brings him or her much closer to the poet and suggests that poetry is something we might want to emphasize more in our training programs. What we are after is not only understanding but capturing this new knowledge in a form that will not let it go away. This means something more than the old shopworn cliche; the language has to be tuned to the patient's ear, word sense and level of discourse. And I think there may be something about the rightness of the formulation that also adds to our sense of 'Yes, that must be right'. The right words should take our breath away, much as they do when we read them in a poem or popular song.

So my point is that even though there is a danger of being fooled by an over-zealous author into believing things that never happened, we are beginning to learn some clues that will help us distinguish good and bad history. To show how far we've come in this respect, I want to read you excerpts from another one of our classic papers to show how much we have changed in our view of the relevance of evidence for understanding:

> *Let me start with a schematic example. It concerns an experience which, though not frequent, is familiar to all analysts. And it is one welcome to all. I mean 'the good analytic hour.' Its course is varied, and I offer only an abstraction from experiences well advanced in analytic therapy. Many a time the 'good hour' does not start propitiously. It may come gradually into its own, say after the first ten or fifteen minutes, when some recent experience has been recounted, which may or may not refer to yesterday's session. Then a dream may come, and associations, and all begin to make sense.*
>
> *In particularly fortunate instances a memory from the near or distant past, or suddenly one from the dark days may present itself with varying degrees of affective charge. At times new elements are introduced as if they had always been familiar, so well do they fit into the scheme of things. And when the analyst interprets, sometimes all he needs to say can be put into a question. The patient may well do the summing up by himself, and himself arrive at conclusions.*
>
> Kris 1956, pp445-455

What I want to point out to start with is the absence of any clinical observation; the details remain just out of sight. The memory from the 'near or distant past' is left vague and undescribed; the 'affective charge' is left unstated; and the way in which all the pieces fit together into the 'scheme of things' and the final summing up by the patient is left to our imagination. But so strong is our need to believe in the probability of a 'good hour' that we are all too willing to listen to another version of this favourite story and become reassured, once again, that every analysis has its share of similar, magical moments.

The description casts a mythic spell because it is presented in the form of a coherent narrative with the classic marks of an uneasy beginning (it 'does not start propitiously') and a happy ending ('the patient may well do the summing up by himself'). It tells a tale we would all like to share; our need to believe tends to disarm our need for more evidence. So artful is the presentation that many readers remember the passage as describing an actual clinical occurrence. In the short space of a well-constructed paragraph, Kris has managed to bring the 'good hour' into being and given it a kind of permanence that does without clinical specimens.

On closer examination, we see that part of its narrative thrust comes from the sense that a single story is being told. The bits and pieces of the analytic hour which may seem random or unexpected at the time later seem (in hindsight) to be part of a continuous narrative thread. Sometimes, I suppose, this kind of continuity really exists; most of the time, it is little more than a rhetorical manoeuvre in the service of the thesis that truly free associations are meaningfully connected and, if left alone, will produce a continuous story.

Something else happens as well during this passage. As you hear about the earmarks of a good hour, you will very likely imagine moments in your own clinical experience that fits Kris' description. Memories are evoked which seem to fit the template of a good hour and I would guess that a kind of re-transcription (*Nachträchlichkeit*) occurs with the result that after reading the Kris paper, these memories now fit slightly better into the overall template. The next time they are remembered, they may even seem to confirm Kris' formulation. But notice that this kind of confirmation is quite different from what is practised in the other sciences.

Which brings me to my second point. Standard theory is repeatedly 'confirmed' by vague and allusive case reports because the allusions can easily remind us of our own, similar experiences which are then readjusted to fit the template. By comparison, a fact-filled case report stands apart from our own experience because of its detail and is more likely to remind us of differences between us and the author.

When we re-read Kris against the perspective I have been trying to develop this afternoon, I think we tend to be somewhat more critical of his mode of presentation. His seamless narrative changes from being reassuring to question-begging; the absence of examples begins to arouse our suspicions. Can we really accept his conclusion as stated or would we like to see for ourselves? Exactly how frequent is the 'good hour' and how often do we find such a sequence in the analyst's verbatim notes? How much is the 'good hour' paper governed by the wish to see analytic process in a particular continuous manner that turns what seems random into something that has a central theme with beginning, middle and end?

IMPLICATIONS FOR THE FUTURE

Countless analysts have commented (usually in private) about how often they feel bewildered by the happenings of a given hour and how frequently they feel at a loss to explain what the patient is doing and how and why he or she moves from one topic to the next. But little of this bewilderment ever finds its way into published clinical reports; on the contrary, they usually present us with a sense of an all-knowing therapist who finds meaning in everything and is only waiting for the proper moment to intervene. There is little room provided for 'I don't know' or other admissions of honesty, and all too often our sense of what course the treatment took is projected back onto the material. As a result, we fool ourselves into thinking that the first dream of treatment foreshadowed its major themes, or that an interchange in hour 457 marked the beginning of a long-lasting negative transference.

Backshadowing not only does a disservice to the material by generating spurious cause-and-effect links; it also blinds us to what Bernstein has called the Principle of Insufficient Cause. This principle refers to the true randomness of everyday life (and of probably a good deal of what goes for free association) and to ways in which significant outcomes are often the result of accidents and miscalculations. This rule not only applies to daily events; it probably applies as well to the timing and outcome of specific interventions. An interpretation may produce a fortunate and productive response for entirely fortuitous reasons, but in our haste to understand everything, this piece of random behaviour is never reported.

At the same time, it is also clear that we can never find a way to present 'just the facts' and a dreary catalogue of sheer utterances - some kind of archival report - will never be published, much less read. Narrative smoothing is clearly necessary as a way to normalise the clinical account in order to make it readable and accessible to an outsider. But how do we protect against the contamination of observation by theory and guard against the distortion of evidence to make it seem more in line with received understandings?

One answer is to assume a largely pragmatic stance toward the problem (see Kirschner 1996) and take the position that case reports should be read as partial interpretations of the clinical material which necessarily blend both facts and theory into a readable account. Some readers will be persuaded by the new mixture and will seek to apply it to their own cases; some sessions (and some patients) will be improved by the result. What works gets talked about, written up, and (sooner or later) taught to new generations of clinicians; what does not work tends to be forgotten. What matters is the effect on the patient and in particular, the relation between what was said and the patient's response. Here is a place for more careful and precise reporting and perhaps we need to encourage more concern with what made the difference as opposed to whether or not the clinical happening conformed to theory. The good hour then becomes an account of one or more specific interventions and the reasons they worked, rather than a celebration of standard theory (as in Kris's paper) with no supporting examples. When there are examples, as in Almond's paper, they would be more useful if they focused on the way in which one of Almond's virtues (e.g. curiosity) uncovered a particular piece of the patient's world view which had been missing up to that moment. For the link to be convincing, we would like to see an example of how the analyst's curiosity was played out in the clinical material and how it elicited a new piece of information from the patient.

This way of looking at case studies treats the published report as a necessary mixture of fact and hypothesis, the first coming from true memories of the clinical event and the second coming from what is unwittingly added to make the story believable and persuasive and in keeping with the commonly accepted paradigm. The hypotheses are tested by the readers as they take what seems useful from the published account and apply it to their own patients. If the new moves succeed, they generate new accounts, also balanced between fact and fiction, and the cycle is repeated. Validation comes in the doing; each new application of a provisional method becomes a one-trial experiment and as the new procedure is successively applied to new patients, it is subtly adjusted to become more effective and efficient. But the emphasis is on the provisional and hypothetical nature of the central propositions (this point gets lost in Almond's presentation).

As clinical reports become more specific and more focused on the particular wording of an invention or on the exact nature of the patient's response, the way is open to mine the riches of our literature with a computer-based search engine. If we are interested in the effect of A on B, we could call up all known instances of A and then study the extent to which they eventuate in B. This possibility argues for the routine archiving of all clinical papers along with the development of a standard vocabulary to describe the more frequent clinical incidents.

If the gains are promising, the drawbacks are also clear. Because each experiment stands alone with no matching control, we never know for sure whether success stems from the new procedure - the specific A/B link - or from one or more unidentified variables; in more technical language, how much is necessary and how much is contingent? Because we can never eliminate the latter, it follows that progress will be uneven and difficult to measure. It is also apparent that precise description is everything; unless the new procedure is accurately described and clearly linked to its clinical response, the clinician/reader will not be persuaded to apply it to his or her own cases.

Finding a way to turn our clinical experience into a useful (and largely accurate) literature depends to a large extent on turning each clinician into a careful observer who is skilled at presenting clinical happenings in unambiguous, sometimes poetic, descriptive language. Special training may be needed to help clinicians to strip away unnecessary jargon and learn not to hide behind standard phrases. But even though the new procedures may be difficult to apply, their benefits are clear. By returning the focus to the clinical impact of a specific intervention or clinical stance, we protect ourselves from the easy slide from hypothesis to conclusion which has bedevilled far too many of our more popular papers. We learn to detect lapses in reasoning, the replacement of evidence for proposition, the use of convention as a brief for evidence, and the doubtful tendency for ought to turn into is. And we begin to generate a literature the truly builds on itself.

Bibliography

Almond, R. (1995) 'The analytic role' *Journal of the American Psychoanalytic Association* 43, pp469-494.

Coleman, D.J. (unpub.) *Narrative performance mode of discourse.*

Grünbaum, A. (1984) *The Foundations of Psychoanalysis.* Berkeley: Univ. of California Press.

Kirschner, S.R. (1996) *The Religious and Romantic Origins of Psychoanalysis.* Cambridge: Cambridge Univ. Press.

Klumpner, G.H. and A. Frank (1991) 'On methods of reporting clinical material' *Journal of the American Psychoanalytic Association* 39, p537-551.

Kris, E. (1956) 'On some vicissitudes of insight' *International Journal of Psycho-Analysis* 37, pp445-455.

Kubie, L. (1958) 'Research into the process of supervision in psychoanalysis' *Psychoanalytic Quarterly* 27, pp226-236.

Masson, J.M. (1985) *The Complete Letters of Sigmund Freud to Wilhelm Fliess: 1887-1904* Cambridge, Mass: Harvard Univ. Press.

Spence, D.P. (1987) *The Freudian Metaphor* New York: W.W. Norton.

Tuckett, D. (1993) 'Some thoughts on the presentation and discussion of clinical material in psychoanalysis' *International Journal of Psycho-Analysis* 74, pp1175-1190.

ABOUT THE CONTRIBUTORS

RONALD BRITTON is a Training Analyst of the British Psycho-Analytical Society and former chairman of the Children and Families Department, Tavistock Clinic. He teaches and lectures widely abroad. In addition to his work on central psychoanalytic subjects he has written on creative writing and on such authors as Wordsworth, Blake and Rilke.

SUSAN BUDD is a psychoanalyst in full-time private practice. She is a member of the British Psycho-Analytical Society and on the Editorial Board of the *International Journal of Psychoanalysis*. Previously a lecturer in Sociology at the London School of Economics, her publications include *Sociologists and Religion* (1972), *Varieties of Unbelief* (1976), and (with Ursula Sharma) *The Healing Bond* (1994).

JULIA BOROSSA is a historian of psychoanalysis. After studying Film and Communications and Comparative Literature at McGill University, she completed a PhD in the History and Philosophy of Science at Cambridge. She has written and lectured on the history and theory of psychoanalysis; gender and sexuality; and literary theory.

LAURENCE SPURLING was a social worker before training as a psychotherapist at the Philadelphia Association. He is a member of the Guild of Psychotherapists, a part-time lecturer in counselling at Birkbeck College and a supervisor at the Red Admiral Project (HIV and Aids counselling). He is Series Editor for the 'Makers of Modern Psychotherapy' published by Routledge, and editor of *From the words of my mouth: Tradition in psychotherapy* (1992).

DONALD SPENCE is a psychoanalyst and former Professor of Psychiatry at the Robert Wood Johnson Medical School, New jersey. He has been concerned for many years with the scientific status of psychoanalysis, explored in such books as *Narrative Truth and Historical Truth* (1982), *The Freudian Metaphor* (1988), and *The Rhetorical Voice of Psychoanalysis* (1994).

IVAN WARD is the Director of Education at the Freud Museum London, and a part-time lecturer in Communications at London Guildhall University.